Cambridge E

Elements in Ancient Philosophy
edited by
James Warren
University of Cambridge

PLATO'S *ION*

Poetry, Expertise, and Inspiration

Franco V. Trivigno
University of Oslo

CAMBRIDGE
UNIVERSITY PRESS

CAMBRIDGE
UNIVERSITY PRESS

University Printing House, Cambridge CB2 8BS, United Kingdom

One Liberty Plaza, 20th Floor, New York, NY 10006, USA

477 Williamstown Road, Port Melbourne, VIC 3207, Australia

314–321, 3rd Floor, Plot 3, Splendor Forum, Jasola District Centre,
New Delhi – 110025, India

79 Anson Road, #06–04/06, Singapore 079906

Cambridge University Press is part of the University of Cambridge.

It furthers the University's mission by disseminating knowledge in the pursuit of
education, learning, and research at the highest international levels of excellence.

www.cambridge.org
Information on this title: www.cambridge.org/9781108713450
DOI: 10.1017/9781108581875

© Franco V. Trivigno 2020

This publication is in copyright. Subject to statutory exception
and to the provisions of relevant collective licensing agreements,
no reproduction of any part may take place without the written
permission of Cambridge University Press.

First published 2020

A catalogue record for this publication is available from the British Library.

ISBN 978-1-108-71345-0 Paperback
ISSN 2631-4118 (online)
ISSN 2631-410X (print)

Cambridge University Press has no responsibility for the persistence or accuracy of
URLs for external or third-party internet websites referred to in this publication
and does not guarantee that any content on such websites is, or will remain,
accurate or appropriate.

Plato's *Ion*

Poetry, Expertise, and Inspiration

Elements in Ancient Philosophy

DOI: 10.1017/9781108581875
First published online: October 2020

Franco V. Trivigno
University of Oslo
Author for correspondence: franco.trivigno@ifikk.uio.no

Abstract: This Element defends an interpretation of Plato's *Ion* on which its primary concern is with audience reception of poetry. The dialogue countenances and rejects two models of poetic reception, the expertise model and the inspiration model, both of which make the audience entirely passive in relation to poetry; and it presents the character of Ion as a comedic figure, a self-ignorant fool whose foolishness is a function of his passive relation to Homer. In the end, I argue that, for Plato, critical engagement is the proper way for audiences to treat poetry. This view holds open the possibility that poetry may express some truths without thereby endorsing the idea that poets are experts who have authoritative knowledge.

Keywords: Plato, *Ion*, poetry, interpretation, comedy

© Franco V. Trivigno 2020

ISBNs: 9781108713450 (PB), 9781108581875 (OC)
ISSNs: 2631-4118 (online), 2631-410X (print)

Contents

1 Introduction

Plato's *Ion* depicts a conversation between Socrates and Ion, a rhapsode who has just arrived in Athens from Epidaurus, where he won first place in a rhapsodic contest.[1] A rhapsode, literally a 'song-stitcher,' is a traveling performer, who recites or performs scenes from poetry and, as Ion is eager to emphasize, gives speeches that interpret or present the meaning of the poetry. Early rhapsodes played the lyre while they sang, as in Figure 1, while later ones carried a staff, as in Figure 3 (on p. 37). Together Socrates and Ion discuss the nature of Ion's profession, rhapsody, as well as the nature of poetry, trying to determine whether it is expertise or divine inspiration that explains success in these domains.

Central to understanding the philosophical stakes of the *Ion* is a set of cultural assumptions about the educational role of poetry and about Homer's prominence amongst the poets. Poetry was thought to be a repository of both technical and ethical knowledge.[2] This might strike us as somewhat peculiar, but in oral cultures, poetry provides an easy way of codifying, memorizing, and passing on practical and cultural information. In Plato's time, Homer was still widely memorized and played a significant role in education, even though literacy and specialized crafts were well established.[3] In Xenophon's *Symposium*, for example, one of the guests, Niceratus, says: "My father was anxious to see me develop into a good man so he made me memorize all of Homer; and so even now I can repeat the whole *Iliad* and the *Odyssey* by heart" (3.6). On the basis of knowing Homer, he claims to know "the art of the estate manager, the political leader, and the general" (4.6). Ion assumes, like many of his contemporaries, that poetry is a source of knowledge and wisdom and that Homer's work contained the greatest store of wisdom. If poets are sources of wisdom and rhapsodes are experts on poetry, then it might be reasonable to think of rhapsodes as having expertise.

One of Plato's philosophical aims throughout his career is to undermine the traditional idea of the poets as sources of wisdom. The *Ion*'s approach is distinctive in several ways. While Plato also treats poetry and performance in the *Republic* and the *Laws*, only the *Ion* features rhapsody so prominently. This is significant since the rhapsode embodies three perspectives on poetry at once: the performer, the

---

[1] The dialogues of Plato are historical fictions usually involving known individuals, though we have no independent evidence about a rhapsode named Ion. The dialogues are also usually dated to a period within Socrates' lifetime; in the case of the *Ion*, scholars generally agree on a dramatic date before 412. See Moore (1974); Murray (1996, 96); Rijksbaron (2007, 1–2).

[2] On oral culture's reliance on song, see Havelock (1963, 36–60); on Homer as a repository of knowledge, see Havelock (1963, 61–86).

[3] While modern scholars debate whether there was such a person as Homer, as opposed to a series of bards, the ancients took it for granted that a single individual composed the *Odyssey* and the *Iliad*.

Figure 1 Rhapsode with lyre. The Metropolitan Museum of Art, New York,
Fletcher Fund, 1956.

interpreter, and the critic. Further, since people commonly memorized, recited, and
appealed to poetry themselves,[4] the rhapsode may be seen as a professionalized
version of the audience. While we see poetic interpretation enacted and its role in
education discussed in the *Hippias Minor* and the *Protagoras*, only the *Ion* explores
the epistemic conditions that make both interpretation and critical evaluation of
poetry possible. The theme of the divine inspiration of poets is discussed or
mentioned in several dialogues (*Phaedrus*, *Apology*, *Meno*, *Timaeus*, and *Laws*),
but the account in the *Ion* is distinctive both for its poetic and fanciful manner of
articulation and for its exaggerated description of the poet's passivity when
composing. Plato discusses the nature of expertise in many dialogues (including
Laches, *Gorgias*, *Phaedrus*, *Euthyphro*, *Republic*, and *Statesman*), but the *Ion*
articulates a distinctive and explicit statement of an epistemological principle for
differentiating forms of knowledge. The *Ion* is similar in style to the shorter
dialogues in which Socrates refutes a reputed expert, like Hippias, Euthyphro,
and Euthydemus, exposing them as foolish and self-ignorant, but Ion is the only
one whose epistemic claims are so closely tied to the wisdom of Homer.[5]

---

[4] See Halliwell (2000) on the cultural practice of citing poetry and Plato's own extensive citation of
poetry.
[5] Cp. Xen. *Mem.* 4.2.10, *Symp.* 3.6, where rhapsodes are denounced as "foolish."

The dialogue treats a number of philosophical issues that are highly relevant for us today. First, there is still nowadays a cultural assumption that great literature, great art, and even great film have something to teach their audience about ethics, human nature, and life in general. In short, many people think that we can learn important truths from the works of (for example) Jane Austen, Henrik Ibsen, and Toni Morrison, and Plato's analysis shines critical light on such claims.[6] Second, reacting emotionally to fiction is a familiar experience for most of us. We may cry, become nervous, and feel joy from reading Tolstoy's *Anna Karenina* or watching von Trier's *Breaking the Waves*. This is puzzling: Why do we have real emotional responses to people and events we know to be fictional? How *can* we? Plato's *Ion* contains the earliest articulation of the so-called paradox of fiction,[7] suggesting these reactions are deeply irrational. Third, the dialogue's concern with poetry is connected to a series of epistemological questions about the legitimacy of epistemic authority, the nature and structure of expertise, and the proper methodology for acquiring knowledge. All of these are important, indeed pressing, questions at a time when the legitimacy of science is being called into question and scientific expertise is needed to deal with a number of looming global crises.

A brief summary of the *Ion* is in order. The dialogue can be divided into five scenes: In the opening scene (530a–d), Socrates praises Ion for having the enviable expertise of rhapsody, and Ion boasts about his skill and accomplishments. Then, Socrates tries to get Ion to specify the nature of his expertise (531a–533d), and the latter is unable to explain what knowledge of Homer amounts to, or how he could have such knowledge without also knowing other poets like Hesiod. In the dialogue's central scene (533e–536d), Socrates proposes an entirely different sort of explanation for Ion's exclusive abilities with respect to Homer: On this picture, Homer is divinely inspired by the Muse, Ion is in turn inspired by Homer, and neither of them possesses expertise. After Ion rejects this account, Socrates and Ion return to the assumption that Ion possesses expertise (536e–541e), but again Ion struggles to make clear what the nature and scope of his expertise is, finally claiming to have learned generalship from Homer. In the end (541e–542b), Socrates presents Ion with a choice: either he is knowledgeable and unjust, for refusing to explain his expertise, or he is not an expert but rather divine. Ion chooses the latter.

Plato's *Ion* has been the subject of scholarly controversy for centuries across several dimensions: (1) the portrayal of Ion; (2) the meaning of its central passage on divine inspiration; and (3) whether the dialogue offers a positive view at all.

---

[6] See Urmson (1982, 133–134).   [7] Radford (1975) is seminal for the modern debate.

First, scholarly discontent has surrounded the character of Ion, who is thought to possess, in Goethe's words, "incredible stupidity" and to whom it is hardly worth dedicating a whole dialogue. The portrayal has a generally comedic feel to it, and this makes scholars confused and angry. The most extreme reaction, common in the nineteenth century, was to declare the dialogue to be spurious.[8] There are two issues here: the philosophical quality of the dialogue's arguments and the dialogue's critical target. First, Ion's alleged stupidity is thought to compromise the arguments and diminish the philosophical value of the discussion. He misses opportunities to resist Socrates' arguments that scholars have found to be obvious. On my reading, Ion's commitment to his own importance and to the great value of his knowledge of Homer makes him unable to see those objections. Indeed, the portrayal of Ion as self-ignorant actually enriches the arguments and is crucial to understanding the philosophical significance of the dialogue.[9] Second, scholars have asserted that, since rhapsodes are unworthy opponents,[10] the dialogue must have some other 'real' topic, and a number of replacements have been proposed: sophists (Flashar 1958), poets (Murray 1996), poetic criticism (LaDrière 1951), poetical inspiration (Tigerstedt 1969), and art (Dorter 1973).[11] Scholars have wrongly thought both that rhapsody cannot be relevant and that there has to be a single exclusive topic.[12] On my view, the fact that Ion is a rhapsode is crucially important to the dialogue, and the relational triad of poet-rhapsode-audience is the dialogue's central concern. It is, in short, about models of poetic reception, that is, how audiences are to respond to poetry and poetic performances.

The second controversy concerns the status of the central passage apparently celebrating poets as divinely inspired. Commentators like the late ancient Neoplatonist Proclus; the Italian Renaissance scholar Marsilio Ficino; and German Romantics like Schelling have read this passage as Plato's genuine celebration of the great value of poetry. On the other hand, many scholars have read the passage as polemical in nature, aiming to mock poets and rhapsodes.

---

[8] The most prominent athetizers were Schleiermacher, Ast, Zeller, and Wilamowitz. The current consensus is that the dialogue is Plato's, with Thesleff (2009, 367–369), as a notable exception. Though stylometrical analyses have proved inconclusive, scholars generally assume an early date of composition, often taking the dialogue to be philosophically immature (Moore 1974, 421, 425). However, several scholars have placed the *Ion* later in Plato's career: see Moore's survey (1974, 421–2n.5) and, most recently, Rijksbaron (2007, 3–8). I make no assumptions about the dialogue's date of composition, since I think that doing so often unduly prejudices interpretations.

[9] Cp. Trivigno (2016) for a similar analysis of Hippias' character.

[10] Some scholars claim that rhapsodes had a reputation for stupidity, but all such arguments are circular, treating Xen. *Symp.* (3.5–6, 4.6–7) as independent evidence. Xenophon's discussion is either indebted to the *Ion* – there are several reminiscences – or to a common source, as Thesleff speculates (2009, 369).

[11] See LaDrière (1951, 26–29) for further discussion.

[12] Against the idea that a dialogue needs a single topic, see Trivigno (2009b).

I argue that the passage is, first and foremost, a comedic parody – an absurdly exaggerated version – of the way the poets thought of themselves. That said, the sheer number of times the idea of poetic inspiration is mentioned in the dialogues suggests that there is, according to Plato, some truth in the idea. In short, I argue that the inspiration story *as stated* in the dialogue ought to be distinguished from the inspiration story *as it might be restated*. The former is a parody, while the latter may well be Plato's real view.

Third, scholars disagree about whether the dialogue offers a positive view of poetry and rhapsody. The dialogue does not, strictly speaking, end in *aporia* but rather with an endorsement of the inspiration story. Some scholars have argued that, since the inspiration account cannot be taken seriously, its final assertion is just another way of rejecting the expertise model. One might compare this ending to that of the *Meno*, in which Socrates seemingly concludes that virtue is a "divine gift" (100b2–3), though there are strong reasons to doubt that this is his real view. Like the *Meno*, the *Ion* is typically classified along with the aporetic dialogues. There are, broadly speaking, two approaches to such dialogues: some see their purpose as clearing away false views without offering any positive solution, whereas others think that one finds at least the seeds of a positive solution. I incline towards an exploratory version of the latter view, which sees the dialogues as testing out philosophical ideas and encouraging readers to think with and beyond what is explicitly offered. Thus, I claim that a positive view about poetic reception can be articulated that is consistent with the arguments of the *Ion* but does not directly follow from them.

My interpretation of the dialogue is focused on two rival models for understanding the relation between the poet, the rhapsode, and audience: what I call 'the expertise model' and 'the inspiration model.' Each model seems to exclude the defining feature of the other: the expertise model is focused on the epistemic content of poetry to the exclusion of its beauty, whereas the inspiration model is focused on the divinely inspired beauty of poetry to the exclusion of its content. A core secondary aim is to understand how the dramatic interplay between Socrates and Ion contributes to the philosophical meaning of the dialogue. I first analyze the dialogue's opening scene in Section 2 to show how it raises the main philosophical questions and dramatic themes of the conversation. In Section 3, I articulate and examine the expertise model, on which poetry and rhapsody are forms of expertise; I argue that the upshot of these arguments is, first, that Ion has no expertise and, second, that rhapsody cannot be an expertise. Then, in Section 4, I present a reading of the passage articulating the inspiration model, on which divine inspiration explains poetic and rhapsodic success, as a parody of poets' self-understanding. I then compare the way that each model understands the notion of 'beauty,' *to kalon*, in Section 5, arguing that neither represents what Plato thinks of as real or genuine beauty. Turning to the dialogue's drama in Section 6, I provide an analysis of Plato's presentation of Ion as comedic imposter, or *alazōn*, and Socrates as ironist, or *eirōn*. I argue that Socrates' ironic praise serves to structure Ion's knowledge-claims and that the exposure of Ion is aimed at showing that his foolish character is a function of his misguided epistemic commitments with respect to poetry. Finally, in Section 7, I try to think beyond the dialogue's explicit content and lay out the core components of what I call the 'critical engagement model'; I claim that it is compatible with the content of some poetry being divinely inspired and that it allows for the possibility of knowledge-based poetry. My interpretation of the *Ion* is distinctive in that it integrates the comedic aspects with the philosophical content, makes philosophical sense of the portrayal of Ion, offers a new account of Socratic irony, and proposes a novel way of understanding the philosophical upshot of the dialogue.

2 The Opening Scene

The opening scene of the *Ion* (530a–d) introduces the dialogue's core philosophical themes – about poetry and rhapsody, knowledge and beauty, and performance and interpretation – and sets up the dramatic interplay between Socrates and Ion.[13]

The dialogue begins with a little vignette establishing the rapport between Ion and Socrates. Ion is well-traveled, boastful, and keen on praise, whereas Socrates presents himself as an enthusiastic supporter, who admires Ion and wishes him well:

> You know, I've often envied you rhapsodes, Ion, for your craft (*technē*). Not only is it always fitting for you to dress up your bodies in order to appear as beautiful (*kallistois*) as you can, it is at the same time necessary for you to spend your time with the poets: many good ones, but most especially Homer, who is the best and most divine poet. And you have to learn not just the man's verses but his thought (*dianoia*) as well – that is enviable! No one could ever become a good rhapsode if he did not understand what the poet is saying. The rhapsode must be an interpreter (*hermēnea*) of the poet's thoughts for the audience, and it is impossible to do this beautifully (*kalōs*) without understanding what the poet says. All of this then is worthy of envy. (530b5–c6)[14]

Could Socrates really mean all of this? Most scholars take Socrates' repeated insistence that he envies rhapsodes to be ironic and in line with the praise he

---

[13] Plato's opening scenes often have this function. See e.g. Trivigno (2011a); Procl. *In Prm.* 658–659.

[14] Translations of the *Ion* are from Woodruff's in Cooper (1997), with minor emendations.

heaps on figures like Euthyphro and Hippias, but there is deep disagreement about what it means to say that Socrates is being ironic.

On my interpretation, which I will elaborate and defend more fully in Section 6, Plato borrows and adapts Aristophanes' techniques of character-ization, placing Ion in the role of *imposter*, that is, one who presents himself as important and deserving of rewards, and Socrates in the role of *ironist*, that is, one who, under a mask of friendly solicitousness, attempts to expose the imposter as a fraud.[15] Plato's imposter, unlike Old Comedy's, is fooled by his own pretensions;[16] his ironist, unlike Old Comedy's, actually aims to help and improve the interlocutor. I have argued extensively that Plato adapts the ironist-imposter device in his presentation of intellectual charla-tans as rivals to Socrates and philosophy.[17] In the typical Platonic encoun-ter, the imposter is ironically praised, the praise elicits claims to wisdom, such claims are undermined and the imposter is exposed as a self-ignorant fool.

Socrates' short speech is exuberant in its ironic praise, and Ion responds as one expects of an imposter: taking Socrates' account to be incredibly flattering, he endorses it wholeheartedly and boasts that he is the best rhapsode who has ever lived:

> That's true, Socrates. For me it's the interpretive part of the craft (*technēs*) that required the most work, and I think I speak more beautifully (*kallion*) about Homer than anyone else. Neither Metrodorus of Lampsacus nor Stesimbrotus of Thasos nor Glaucon nor anyone else past or present could declaim as many beautiful thoughts (*kalas dianoias*) about Homer as I can. (530c7–d3)

Socrates' strategy is successful in eliciting an explicit claim to knowledge in connection with Ion's favored poet, Homer. As we will see, Ion will spend the entire dialogue attempting to articulate and defend this claim against Socrates' skeptical questioning. When Socrates asks for a "demonstration" (530d5) of his interpretive abilities, this prompts even further boasting from Ion:

> Really, Socrates, it's worth hearing how well I've adorned (*kekosmēka*) Homer. I think I'm worthy of being crowned with a golden crown by the Sons of Homer! (530d6–8)

---

[15] See Ranta (1967).
[16] See Socrates' description in the *Apology*: "I thought that he appeared wise to many people and *especially to himself*, but he was not" (21c5–7).
[17] See Trivigno (2012a, 2012b, 2016, 2017).

The Sons of Homer were a Homeric guild claiming descent from Homer, and Ion claims to deserve even more victories, accolades and financial rewards. Socrates immediately puts off the demonstration for some other time and pivots to a philosophical question about the nature and scope of Ion's alleged expertise.

Socrates' irony plays an important role in the dialogue, bringing out an ethical dimension to the critique of the epistemic value of rhapsody. It reveals something about Ion's self-knowledge, or more to the point, his self-ignorance, since Socrates exposes the gap between how Ion thinks of himself and who he really is. Socrates' ironic praise is also philosophically crucial both in laying out several of the premises that guide the ensuing discussion and in indicating some of the tensions in the notion of rhapsody that come to the fore in the dialogue. The claim that rhapsody is a craft is central to the expertise model. The Greek word for 'craft' is *technē*, and this term picks out forms of expertise ranging from carpentry to mathematics.[18] It usually indicates a profession that ranges over a particular domain and involves a specialized methodology. In several dialogues (though not in the *Ion*), Plato has Socrates argue that virtue is a craft, or at least very much like a craft (see e.g. *Euthyphro* 13a–14b, *Laches* 184e–185e, and *Charmides* 165c–e). The beautiful appearance of the rhapsode, praised here by Socrates, is central to the inspiration model. The Greek term for 'beautiful' is *kalos*, and this wide term covers everything from physical appearance to nobility of character. The adverbial form, *kalōs*, is usually translated as 'well'; but 'beautifully' preserves the linguistic resonance. The beauty of poetry and rhapsodic performance is a crucial theme of the dialogue, in particular the potential gap between seeming beautiful and really being beautiful.

The centrality of Homer in Socrates' description is no accident, since it was Homer above all who was credited as "the man who educated Greece" (*Rep.* 606e2). Thus, if Plato is to take up philosophy's fight against the ethical and epistemic authority of poets, it is Homer that needs to be unseated. Socrates' designation of Homer as the "most divine" (530b10) poet is also an implicit gesture towards the inspiration model, since that model makes the gods the ultimate source of poetic beauty. Homer's primacy is connected to the enormous scope of his writings, and thus the apparently unlimited range of his 'thought.'[19] This is important for the expertise model and for understanding Ion's avowedly *exclusive* interest in Homer (531a3–4): if Homer is an expert about everything, and one is an expert about Homer, then one might think that one already possesses all the knowledge there is to have.

Socrates' description of rhapsody indicates that he sees it as comprising two main activities: (1) the recitation and performance of a poet's verses and (2)

---

[18] See LSJ, s.v.   [19] Cp. Xen. *Symp.* 4.6

the interpretation and evaluation of a poet's thought. Both activities require that the rhapsode understand "what the poet is saying," and both are ways for the rhapsode to communicate the poet's thought to an audience. The 'thought' or epistemic content of poetry concers how to perform various crafts or skills, or more generally, how to act ethically and live a good life. Rhapsody has, then, a certain structure, with an epistemic core, two methods, and a common goal. One might object to my taking performance and interpretation to be parallel activities. Shouldn't the rhapsode's interpretation be subordinate to his performance? The most straightforward evidence for denying this is that Ion himself foregrounds his role as interpreter (*hermēneus*), as opposed to performer, in response to Socrates' praise, and he is eager to demonstrate his interpretive skills.[20] The term, *hermēneus*, is derived from the name of Hermes (*Hermēs*), who was the gods' messenger, and it is the origin of the English word 'hermeneutics,' or the art of interpretation. The rhapsodes were not sophists and should not be confused with them, but their interpretive task put them directly in competition with sophists, who gave speeches interpreting and evaluating poetry and thought understanding poetry was central to education (cp. *Hip. Min.*; *Prt.* 339a–347d). Plato has the sophist Protagoras declare that "the greatest part of a man's education is to be clever about poetry, that is, the ability to understand the words of the poets, to know when a poem is correctly composed and when not, and to know how to analyze a poem and to respond to questions about it" (*Prt.* 338e6–339a3).[21] Thus, rhapsodes contended with the sophists for the legacy of the poets and the claim to wisdom that they enjoyed.

When Ion first articulates in his own words what is valuable about his interpretive abilities, he claims that he speaks "more beautifully (*kallion*) about Homer than anyone else" and that he expresses "many beautiful thoughts (*kalas dianoias*)" about Homer. This might seem puzzling. Ion does not say that his thoughts about Homer are true or even that Homer's thoughts are true. What makes these thoughts beautiful, and what notion of beauty is Ion operating with? Ion claims that his speeches "adorn" Homer, but again it is not clear how exactly to understand this. Will his interpretation praise Homer, who will then seem even more beautiful? Will it improve Homer somehow? I tackle the question of how to understand what it is to be 'beautiful' – or *kalos* – directly in Section 5. There I also take up the question of how beauty is understood very differently on the expertise and inspiration models respectively.

In sum, Socrates' ironic praise lays the groundwork for two ways of understanding what is praiseworthy about Ion and rhapsody. Socrates first offers the

---

[20] *Pace* Dorter (1973, 68). On the rhapsodic tradition of interpretation, see Richardson (2006).
[21] See Trivigno (2013).

expertise model, making Ion a praiseworthy poetry expert, and then offers the
inspiration model, praising Ion as divinely inspired, but Ion ends up rejecting
each in turn. At the end of the dialogue, Ion is praised for having the noble art of
generalship, but Ion abandons this idea too, choosing to be divine and praiseworthy over being a blameworthy expert (542a–b). On my reading, these larger
movements between the expertise model and the inspiration model are best
explained by Ion's desire to be worthy of the praise that Socrates first heaps
on him.

3 The Expertise Model of Poetic Reception

Ion is very eager to give his demonstration, but Socrates, just after asking for
one, demurs and says that he would rather hear whether Ion is an expert only
about Homer. This question begins the first of two long passages trying to
account for Ion and rhapsody according to the expertise model. In this section,
I argue that the expertise model of poetic reception forms the basis of two
arguments: a *reductio ad absurdum* argument concluding that Ion does not
possess a *technē*, that is, an expertise (531a–533d) and a more general argument
concluding that there is no such expertise as rhapsody (536e–541e).[22] The
expertise model is committed to what I will call 'the content thesis' about
poetry, namely that poetry can teach its audience by transmitting true *epistemic
content* to them. Rhapsodic expertise about Homer's poetry is then expertise
about what his poetry can teach us.

3.1 The Content and Scope of Poetry

Socrates first examines the scope or domain of the alleged rhapsodic craft.
Socrates proceeds on the assumption that an expertise has a determinate range
of objects about which it has knowledge (cp. 537c–e; *Grg.* 452a–455d) and that
this scope will be general in nature, picking out a kind rather than individuals.
Thus, Socrates' question about whether Ion is "clever" (531a2) – the Greek
word, *deinos*, carries the same ambiguous connotations in English[23] – "only
about Homer" (531a–2), or also about Hesiod and other poets, is not an entirely
innocent one. Ion thinks that it is "enough" to have expertise about Homer
(531a3), claiming to find discussions of other poets boring (532b–c).

The core question is: What does it mean to have expertise *about* Homer?[24]
Having expertise about Homer is taken to be, or at least include, expertise

---

[22] *Pace* Pappas, who sees the first argument as more general and stronger (1989, 384).

[23] The term is also used in a positive vein: see Protagoras' self-description as "clever" (*Prt.* 338e6–
339a3, quoted in Section 2). Cp. the use of *deinos* in the "ode to man" in Soph. *Ant.* 332–375.

[24] The about-relationship is repeatedly expressed in the Greek by *peri* plus the genitive; see LSJ s.v.

about what Homer "speaks" *about*, that is, the epistemic content of Homer's poetry.[25] This specification of the scope and content of the rhapsodic craft is crucial to the argument of the first section, for it allows Socrates to treat Homer as though he were making claims about the world and Ion's expertise as expertise about those claims. On this picture, Homer's poetry depicts or describes an activity, for example archery, being performed in a certain way, and the lesson or content of the passage is the recommendation that the activity, shooting an arrow at an enemy, be performed in the way it is portrayed or described. Thus, the recommendation is either implicit, in the case of depiction, or explicit, in the case of description and endorsement.[26] Achieving expertise about the relevant passage(s) is thus taken to provide the rhapsode with expertise about the relevant activity, and any proper assessment of the passage will, in turn, require such expertise.[27]

Socrates argues that, given this way of understanding poetic content, Ion cannot maintain his claim to exclusive expertise about Homer. Given that Homer and Hesiod sometimes "say the same thing" (531a5–6), that is, make identical recommendations about a given subject, Ion appears to be in an equally good position to explain the Hesiodic passages. When asked whether he would "explain (*exēgēsaio*) what Homer said better and more beautifully (*kallion*) than what Hesiod said" (531a6–8) in cases of agreement, Ion claims that he would be able to explain both equally well. The emphasis on *explanation* is squarely in line with the interpretive task of setting forth the thought of the poet and communicating what he means. This concession already undercuts his denial that he has expertise on Hesiod, since it turns out that there are "a great many" subjects (531a6) on which Homer and Hesiod say the same thing. Turning to the subjects where Homer and Hesiod both agree and disagree, for example, divination, Socrates asks whether he or an expert diviner would be able to "explain [such passages] better and more beautifully (*kallion*)" (531b5–6). Ion rightly concedes that the diviner would know better, since experts in divination can best explain the *content* of the poetic recommendations. This might seem like a strange concession – how can a diviner be an expert in poetry? – but it is necessary given the way the content of poetry is understood. Of course, a similar argument would be possible for all professions and kinds of expertise.

---

[25] In Greek, *legō*, the word for 'speak,' can indicate both what is actually said and what is meant by what is said (LSJ, s.v. III.9).

[26] The conception of imitation, so prominent in *Republic*, is absent in *Ion*, but it is implied in the expertise model (cp. Dorter 1973, 71; Murray 1992, 34).

[27] A background assumption is that Homer himself possessed the relevant expertise, enabling him to describe and depict such activities accurately (cp. *Rep.* 598d–e).

So far, Ion has claimed to be able to explain the Hesiodic passages that agree with Homer but not the passages that disagree. Socrates now attacks this possibility. In short, Socrates claims that the ability to explain agreements about a certain topic entails the ability to explain disagreements (531b7–9). This is because expertise in the relevant content is necessary for explaining the agreements, but it is also sufficient for explaining disagreements. Ion's claim to be able to explain the agreements between Homer and Hesiod then commits him to being able to explain the disagreements as well. Yet if he can do that, then Ion turns out to be an expert in Hesiod. This completes the first step in the *reductio*, showing that Ion, on pain of contradiction, must possess expertise on, or be "clever" about, Hesiod (531c1).

Socrates then shows that the other poets also "compose about the same subjects" as Homer (531d4–5). This forces Ion to concede that he must also be an expert about "the other poets" (531c2). The account of the content of Homer's poetry is striking both for its high level of generality and for its unlimited scope:

> Doesn't [Homer] mainly go through tales of war, and of how people deal with each other in society – good people and bad, ordinary folks and craftsmen? And of the gods, how they deal with each other and with men? And doesn't he recount what happens in heaven and in hell, and tell of the births of gods and heroes? (531c4–d1)

Notice that Socrates mentions generic people, gods, and wars. This is important, since Homer's educational potential relies on the idea that his depictions of specific people and events are relevant for, and can be applied to, people living in the present. The unrestricted scope of the descriptions is no accident either. In the *Republic*, Socrates mentions those who believe that Homer "knows all the crafts and human matters, virtue as well as vice, and divine matters too" (10.598d7–e2). In short, Socrates' description here is intended to be exhaustive.[28] The argument may be reconstructed thus:

P1   One is an expert about Homer if and only if one is an expert about the subjects of Homer's poetry.

P2   One is an expert about Hesiod if and only if one is an expert about the subjects of Hesiod's poetry.

P3   The subjects of Hesiod's poetry are the same as the subjects of Homer's poetry.

C   Therefore, if one is an expert on Homer's poetry, one is also an expert on Hesiod's poetry.

---

[28] Cp. Xen, *Symp*. 4.6: "You no doubt know that the most wise Homer has expressed practically everything pertaining to humanity."

Since Homer's poetry ranges over everything human and divine, there will not be any poet who cannot be slotted into P2 and P3, since, whatever their subject is, Homer will have it covered. Thus, the line of reasoning will warrant a further conclusion:

C2 If one is an expert on Homer's poetry, one is also an expert on all poets. This second step in the *reductio* further expands the range of poets that Ion is committed to being an expert on, if he really is an expert on Homer.

Understanding poetic content in terms of crafts or other forms of knowledge may seem strange and clearly wrong. Indeed, the biconditionals in P1 and P2 entail that craft practitioners are experts in poetry. Why should anyone think that good archers are experts on poetry about archery? Such skepticism is understandable, but this is simply an implication of the way that the expertise model understands what it means to be an expert about a poet, and it is borne out by Ion repeatedly conceding that the relevant craft experts know better than a rhapsode would about Homeric passages concerning their craft (531b6–7; cp. 538b3, c6, d6). Ion might have evaded Socrates' argument by highlighting aesthetic features of Homer's verse, claiming exclusive expertise on that, but this would severely diminish the alleged educational value of expertise in Homer. It is at the core of Ion's self-image and sense of importance that he is an expert about Homeric *content*.

3.2 Evaluation and the Methodology of Poetry

Ion tries to salvage Homer's uniqueness, and thus worthiness for his special expertise, by claiming that, even though it is true that the poets write about the same topics, Homer writes about these topics "much better" (531d11). Socrates uses mathematics and medicine as test cases for understanding what evaluating one speaker as better than another entails (531d–e).[29] The expert in medicine can discern and judge who "speaks well (*eu*)" (531e1), that is, correctly about medical matters, and who "speaks badly (*kakōs*)" (531e2), that is, incorrectly. In short, "the same person" is able to identify both good and bad and better and worse speakers (531e10).[30] The core philosophical point is that pairs of comparative evaluations entail one another, such that it is impossible for one to judge that A speaks better than B without thereby also judging that B speaks

---

[29] Cp. *Hip. Min.* 366c–367d, where the expert in mathematics is best able to tell the truth and to lie about calculation.

[30] Socrates arguably runs together comparative evaluations – better and worse assessments – and evaluations as good or bad. I do not think that the distinction is important to the argument, since expertise is taken to be necessary for both sets.

worse than A.[31] Thus, the ability to pick out good speakers on a given subject is the same as the ability to pick out bad speakers, and both are a function of understanding the content of what both speakers say. The general lesson may be stated as such:

> One is able to pick out a good speaker on a certain subject if and only if one is able to pick out a bad speaker on that subject.

Socrates applies this general insight to the case of Ion: If he really is able to pick out Homer's poetry as superior to the others on the basis of knowledge, then it must be because he also understands and can explain why the poetry of the others is inferior. He must be an "adequate judge of all who speak on the same subject" (532b5–6) such that if Ion can make comparative evaluations amongst the poets, then he "must be equally clever about Homer and the other poets" (532b3–4).

Of course, the biconditional also warrants an inference in the other direction, that is, from the inability to explain bad speakers to the inability to explain good speakers. When Ion insists that, despite all of Socrates' valiant efforts to prove so, he is so far from being an expert on other poets that he "doze[s] off" whenever other poets are discussed and is "incapable of contributing anything worthwhile" (532c1–2) to the discussion, the other shoe finally drops and Socrates somewhat casually claims that Ion is "unable to speak about Homer on the basis of knowledge or expertise" (532c6–7). This is where Socrates' argument has been leading all along, and here we get a clear statement of it, which is, as befits a *reductio*, the negation of the argument's original assumption. However, this proclamation does not amount to a rejection of the possibility of a rhapsodic expertise as such, since the failure of a single individual to possess an expertise that they claim to have is hardly sufficient for showing that the expertise in question is itself dubious.

When Socrates restates the argument with a focus on what enables comparative evaluations in general, he raises broader questions about the status of rhapsody as an expertise and about artistic criticism, that is, the ability to explain and evaluate fine arts. He begins by assuming that "there is an expertise of poetry as a whole" (532c8–9). Since every form of expertise has "the same methodology throughout" (532d2),[32] so too will poetry employ

---

[31] Such evaluations must be made according to a single criterion, thus eliminating the possibility of evaluating one as better in one respect but worse in another.

[32] The phrase *ho autos tropos tēs skepseōs* means literally 'the same manner of inquiry.' Since it is meant to encompass the learning and the practice of the art, 'methodology' seems better suited as a translation. Woodruff's 'discipline' is a good alternative.

the same methodology.[33] The implication is that someone who can make comparative evaluations about practitioners can do so *because* they know the methodology of the relevant expertise. Painting, sculpture, flute-playing, and cithara-playing each have a single methodology, and those who are in a position to critique and evaluate practitioners can do so based on an understanding of the methodology.[34] Socrates proceeds to show that a critic is able to evaluate and assess *all* practitioners, and not one.[35] If, by analogy, Ion is a critic with knowledge of poetry's methodology, he too should be able to assess all poets. If rhapsody's task is the evaluation of poetry, then it follows from this argument that any rhapsode would know the methodology of the poetic expertise and, on that basis, be able to assess all poets. Ion repeatedly claims that he does not possess expertise about the other poets; thus, it follows that he is incapable of speaking about Homer on the basis of expertise.

This line of argument raises deeper questions about how to characterize the relationship between a critical expertise and the expertise that it judges. In Socrates' descriptions of critics' abilities, he calls them "clever" (532e8, 533b2, 533b8) several times – this may be Plato's subtle way of signaling that such criticisms of fine arts do not really involve expertise. More generally, can one have a critical expertise without having the object-expertise as well? Can one be a painting critic without also being a painter and, if so, how would such an expertise relate to painting? The nature of the relationship between critical expertise and object-expertise, or more generally between first- and second-order expertise, becomes quite pressing in the case of rhapsody and poetry. If rhapsody knows the methodology of poetry when it assesses poetry, how is the expertise of rhapsody distinct from that of poetry itself? Does rhapsody contain, or range over, poetic expertise? How could it do so without violating the principle that each expertise has its own methodology? When Socrates imagines a rhapsody critic, he forces us to consider an even higher order expertise that ranges over rhapsody itself and is able to assess all of its practitioners. How would the expertise of rhapsody-criticism relate to rhapsody itself? These reflections also force us to confront poetry's status as a unified expertise with a particular methodology. Throughout the entire discussion, poetry has been treated

---

[33] This claim should not be interpreted as implausibly narrow. Socrates would surely allow, e.g., that carpentry employs different tools and techniques. The methodology explains why one uses this kind of tool and technique for this kind of construction.

[34] One might object that the existence of different poetic genres and painting styles makes the idea of a single methodology highly implausible. Plato is encouraging us to think of such genres and styles not as independent units with distinctive methodologies but as different tools within a single methodology, parallel to the way that a carpenter might employ different building techniques.

[35] See the argument reconstruction in Janaway (1995, 18–19).

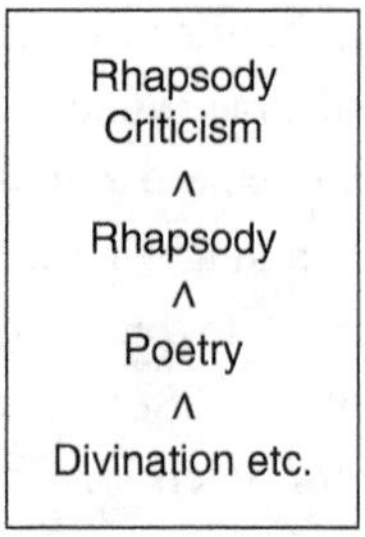

```
┌─────────────────────┐
│     Rhapsody        │
│     Criticism       │
│        ∧            │
│     Rhapsody        │
│        ∧            │
│      Poetry         │
│        ∧            │
│   Divination etc.   │
└─────────────────────┘
```

Figure 2 Implicit hierarchy of expertise.

as though its content were identical to the contents of other forms of expertise, as though being a good poet required knowing all other forms of expertise. If the craft of poetry contains, or ranges over, the expertise of divination, medicine, and so on, how are we to specify the methodology specific to poetry? How are we to understand the relations depicted in Figure 2? When Socrates returns to the expertise model, questions about the boundaries between different forms of expertise are taken up more directly.

3.3 Expertise Revisited: The Principle of Epistemic Distinctness

Ion rejects the initial articulation of the expertise model because he "know[s] about [him]self" that he is able to speak beautifully only about Homer (534c5). The inspiration model is then presented as an alternative that captures the exclusivity of his interest in Homer. I will discuss this model in Section 4, but it is worth noting here that Ion also rejects it because it clashes with his self-understanding (536d). This second round (536e–541e) with the expertise model differs from the first in at least three ways: First, though Ion's expertise is still a theme, the arguments focus more on rhapsody as such. Second, the discussion involves particular passages in Homer, displaying the alleged content of Homer's wisdom. Third, Ion is portrayed as even more foolish and ridiculous.[36] We get two arguments showing that rhapsody is not an expertise. The first (536e–540a) employs a new principle about individuating expertise to show that rhapsody, conceived as knowledge about the expertise of poetry, cannot be an expertise. The second (540b–541e) reveals that rhapsody, conceived as a kind of rhetoric, cannot be an expertise.

When Socrates returns to the expertise model, he reaffirms a core premise of that model, namely the content thesis, and the claim that expertise in Homer is expertise in what Homer's poetry is about. Socrates begins by asking Ion: "on

---

[36] Cp. *Hippias Minor*, which has a comparable structure, returning to arguments closely related to those discussed earlier in the dialogue (366c–369a, 373c–376b).

which of Homer's subjects do you speak well? I don't suppose you speak well on all of them" (536e1–2). Ion enthusiastically asserts his universal expertise on Homer: "I do, Socrates, believe me, on every single one!" (536e3). Socrates here articulates a further criterion for an expertise – what I will call 'the principle of epistemic distinctness' – that explicitly rules out the possibility that a second-order expertise could know the same thing as a first-order expertise over which it ranges. Socrates claims that "god has granted to each craft the ability to know a certain job or function (*ergon*)" (537c5–6). Each expertise is its own independent unit with a sharply restricted domain, in addition to having a distinctive methodology. There is likely a background assumption that the overall structure and organization of knowledge reflect the structure and organization of the world.[37] The principle entails, on Socrates' strict understanding, that there is no overlap at all between any two different forms of expertise. Each expertise has a unique and distinct domain and "what we know (*gignōskomen*) by one expertise, we will not know (*gnōsometha*) by another" (537d2). What one knows by navigation, one does not know by medicine; what one knows by medicine, one does not know by architecture; and so on. If one thinks that the structure of knowledge should map onto the structure of the world, then such a division will seem highly intuitive.[38] Thus, any two epistemic agents who know the same thing will do so in virtue of having and employing the same expertise (537e). Further, the one possessing the relevant expertise – and only such a person – will be able to evaluate whether any action or claim in that domain is correct (538a5–7). This effectively blocks the possibility that a second-order expertise could know the same content and evaluate the same domain, or that any two individual kinds of expertise could account for the same content.

Socrates employs the principle of epistemic distinctness to refute Ion's claim to expertise on all passages in Homer by counterexample: He shows that, for all expertise-relevant passages, it is the relevant expert – a chariot-driver, a doctor, a fisherman, and a diviner – rather than the rhapsode, that has the knowledge to judge them. In my analyses of Socrates' use of these passages, I will try to do three things: show how the passage employs the principle of epistemic distinctness to discredit the rhapsode's ability to judge the passage, examine the context of the passage in Homer's text to see whether and to what extent it might bear on Socrates' use of these examples, and argue that the passages become progressively less appropriate for analysis according to the expertise model.

---

[37] Note that this does not rule out expertise hierarchies in general. It simply rules out hierarchies of the sort that entail an identical content. For example, generalship could govern horsemanship without the general knowing the expertise of the horseman. Cp. *Euthyd.* 290b–d; *Rep.* 601c–e.

[38] Cp. the way knowledge is divided up in, e.g., the *Statesman*.

The first passage (*Il.* 23.335–40) is the most amenable to the expertise model's way of understanding the transmission of knowledge from Homer to his audience. Socrates asks Ion to recite the guidance that Nestor gives to his son, Antilochus, right before a chariot race. It consists in specific direct advice on how to manage the turn, including instructions on bodily positioning, weight distribution, and the use of the reins.[39] Thus, it seems straightforwardly to be a passage that an expert charioteer might be able to evaluate. Turning to the scene in the *Iliad* provides some interesting context to the advice and its repercussions. First, the advice is given in a speech in which the value of "skill" is repeatedly praised as decisive in various domains. Second, the winner of the race, Diomedes, wins because the gods directly intervene by smashing the chariot of his nearest opponent and granting amazing speed to his team. Third, Antilochus comes in second place, using his skills to get past Menelaus, but Antilochus' brinksmanship – he forces Menelaus to pull up to avoid a crash – is deemed both dangerous and a form of cheating by the latter, who is furious when the race ends. Even though the context calls into question the extent to which Homer is actually endorsing the advice of Nestor, Socrates asks whether Homer "speaks correctly (*orthōs*)" (537c1). Given the principle of epistemic distinctness, Ion is forced to agree that a charioteer, rather than a doctor or a rhapsode, would know whether Homer "speaks beautifully (*kalōs*)" (538b2) about charioteering.[40] It is "because he possesses that expertise" (537c3–4), that is, in virtue of being a charioteer, that he is able to judge the passages. In virtue of being a rhapsode, one knows nothing about Homer's charioteering passages.

The second passage (*Il.* 11.630, 639–40) concerns a scene in the *Iliad* in which Hecamede gives "barley-medicine" (538b8) to the wounded Machaon – he has taken an arrow in the shoulder – to drink.[41] Though the passage contains the description of an action, and not direct advice, it is still quite amenable to the expertise model. An expert might approve or disapprove of giving barley-medicine to an injured man, and, indeed, in the *Republic*, Socrates discusses this very passage, claiming that current doctors would not approve of it because barley-medicine causes inflammation (405d–406a). It is clear that a doctor, and not a rhapsode, would know such things. In the context of the *Iliad*, the potion is served to Machaon, a doctor by profession and one of the sons of Asclepius, the god of medicine. Thus, we might say that an expert within the context implicitly approves of the remedy by drinking it without comment. Socrates asks whether a doctor or a rhapsode "would diagnose beautifully (*kalōs*)" whether or not

---

[39] Cp. Xen. *Symp.* 4.6, which references this same passage.

[40] In formulating the central question for the first three passages, Plato plays subtly on the relation between the adverbs *orthōs*, or 'correctly,' and *kalōs*, or 'beautifully.' I return to this in Section 5.

[41] Plato misquotes Homer here, conflating three lines.

"Homer speaks correctly (*orthōs*)" (538c4–5), and it is clear that it is in virtue of the doctor's art, and not the rhapsode's, that one rightly judges such passages.

The third passage (*Il.* 24.80–2) describes the goddess, Iris, diving to the seafloor, using the simile of a weighted fishing hook:

Leaden she plunged to the floor of the sea like a weight
That is fixed to a field cow's horn. Given to the hunt
It goes among ravenous fish, carrying death. (5378c2–3)

This passage seems less amenable to the expertise model precisely because what it actually describes is a swiftly traveling goddess, which the fishing simile is meant to illuminate. Whether or not Iris's descent resembled the descent of a fishing hook would not be within the fisherman's purview, and the fact that fishing hooks bring death to fish is hardly a matter for experts. Still, an expert fisherman might comment on whether bovine horns were used as fishing hooks and whether or not they were weighted, so there is arguably something for the fisherman to say. In the context of the *Iliad*, Iris is rushing down from Olympus to bring Thetis to Zeus, who wants her to persuade her son, Achilles, to return Hector's corpse to the Trojans. Fishing seems hardly relevant to the scene's main concerns. When Socrates asks whether the fisherman or the rhapsode would "judge" whether "Homer speaks beautifully (*kalōs*) or not," Ion thinks it is "clear" that the fisherman's art is the relevant one (538d4–6). Here, we might begin to wonder whether something has gone wrong, since the aesthetic features of the simile are surely most relevant in this passage.

The last two passages concern divination, recalling the dialogue's very first example (531b), and for these Socrates reverses the procedure both by first choosing a craft and then identifying the relevant passages from Homer and by imagining that it is Ion asking Socrates the questions. Socrates claims that he will "easily and truly" be able to answer 'Ion's' question: "which are the passages that belong to a diviner and to divination, passages that he should be able to judge as to whether they are well or badly composed?" (538e2–5). Socrates chooses a passage from the *Odyssey* in which the prophet Theoclymenus has an inspired vision of the suitors' impending deaths (20.351–3, 355–7) and one from the *Iliad* in which an eagle carrying a snake is bitten by and drops it near the Trojan troops (12.200–7).

The *Odyssey* passage is not straightforwardly amenable to the expertise model's way of understanding presence and endorsement of epistemic content. First, Theoclymenus' prediction about the suitors is surely correct, but we do not need a diviner to tell us that, since anyone who knows the story of Odysseus knows that he kills Penelope's suitors. Second, since the seer here is presented as simply the passive recipient of an inspired vision – he does not really *do* anything – it is not clear what the expert seer would evaluate. There is, in short, no gap between the vision and its interpretation; Theoclymenus just "sees" (20.367) the future and does not employ expertise at all.[42] In the *Odyssey*, the scene occurs when Athena has "made [the suitors] wits wander" (20.346), and they hurl food at Odysseus, disguised as a beggar, and laugh excessively at Telemachus. The gods are, in short, directly intervening at multiple levels. In any case, Socrates considers his answer to be clearly correct because it is a direct application of the principle of epistemic distinctness: the assumption that the passage is for a diviner to judge makes it necessarily the case that it is not for the rhapsode to judge.

The *Iliad* passage concerns a very different form of divination, bird-sign interpretation. It was commonly thought that the disposition, placement, and actions of birds were a way for the gods to communicate with mortals. Socrates' passage describes the bird-sign, but not the interpretation, so, by itself, there is nothing for a diviner to assess. However, in the scene in the *Iliad*, the significance of the sign is a matter of deep disagreement. Polydamas, Hector's counselor, claiming to articulate "what a seer would say" (12.228–9), interprets the omen indicating that the Trojans will not return home successful if they attack the Achaean ships, and he thus advises holding back. Hector angrily rejects this interpretation, accusing Polydamas of cowardice, threatening to kill him and castigating bird-sign interpretation as worthless.[43] Hector was visited by the goddess Iris, with a direct message from Zeus, advising him to attack the Achaean ships (11.207–9), and he gives this more direct advice priority. It is genuinely unclear how a bird-sign expert would evaluate Polydamas' interpretation. In one sense, he is clearly right that the Trojans will ultimately fail, like the eagle, to return home having conquered the enemy. On the other hand, it is far from clear that Hector should follow Polydamas' advice and refrain from attacking the ships. Thus, even if we grant that Polydamas has the facts right about the future, it is not clear what the normative or ethical implications of those facts are for Hector's life and character. No bird-sign expert would know how to weigh Polydamas' interpretation, however right, against the direct message from Zeus. Further, Hector's criticism of bird-sign interpretation raises the question of whether it is a kind of expertise at all. However, assuming that it is, this passage clearly falls within the purview of the bird-sign interpreter, and not the rhapsode.

In sum, the application of the principle of epistemic distinctness seems to be devastating for rhapsody's claim to expertise in Homer, since, for every passage

---

[42] Even if Brickhouse and Smith are right in their speculative suggestion that the seer has a *technē* for putting themselves in a state of receptivity (1994, 196–199), it still is not clear how a diviner would evaluate the passage.

[43] Cp. *Phdr.* 244d, where "rational" bird-sign interpretation is unfavorably compared to "mad" inspired vision.

for which there is a relevant expertise, it is in virtue of that expertise and only that expertise that anyone may claim the ability to evaluate and judge that passage. Ion concedes such passages are for the experts to "examine and judge" (539d2–3). Socrates proceeds piecemeal here, to be sure, but since the principle rules out that rhapsody, qua rhapsody, can have expertise in any other form of knowledge whatsoever, there does not seem to be any content left over for rhapsody to be an expertise about. One can easily see that a further application of the principle to poetry itself would rule out the possibility that Homer could know any of the forms of expertise in virtue of being a poet. He might happen to know all different kinds of expertise and be a poet, but he could not know them *because* he is a poet.

The set of passages has also put some pressure on the idea that poetry is the right vehicle for the conveyance of epistemic content in the first place. In short, some passages seem much better suited than others to communicate a recommendation regarding some activity. Indeed, certain passages seem not to be about such content at all: The last three passages contain vivid imagery in scenes of dramatic importance. One might be inclined to insist that it is the aesthetic qualities of the verses that matter and that it really is the rhapsode, and not the fisherman or the doctor, who can evaluate that aspect of Homer's poetry.

3.4 Poetry As Rhetoric

Ion still does not quite get it. When asked to specify the passages that a rhapsode would have expertise about, Ion again says, "all of them!" (539e6). When reminded how the principle of epistemic distinctness made craftsman, and not rhapsodes, experts on craft-relevant passages, Ion tries to set aside these passages as 'merely' exceptions. He has made significant concessions, allowing Socrates essentially to vacate the rhapsodic expertise of content, but he seems not to realize it. In general, he is simply unable to say what exactly the content of his knowledge of Homer amounts to. He reaches then for an alternative sort of answer, one that picks up on the earlier discussion of good and bad speakers and puts rhapsodes again in competition with sophists. He claims, in short, that a rhapsode has a kind of general rhetorical ability, that is, the knowledge of "what is fitting (*prepei*) to say" (540b3).

Ion picks out the societal, interpersonal roles of speakers and not their epistemic roles – their social identity rather than their expertise.[44] He chooses three pairs of social roles: "man" and "woman," "slave" and "freeman," and "leader" and "follower" (540b3–5). Each set is a hierarchical pair and these sets can be

---

[44] Cp. Meno's first attempt to answer 'What is virtue?' by describing a virtue for each social role: man, woman, child, freeman, and slave (*Meno* 71e–72a).

combined in order to place one within the overall social hierarchy, in which, for example, a female slave follower would be the lowest and a free male leader would be the highest. This cross-section of social roles has the advantage of encompassing all of the human speakers in *Iliad* and the *Odyssey* and being relevant categories for fifth-century Greece. This move is clearly meant to evade the previous line of criticism, while at the same time maintaining an appropriately impressive set of Homeric passages for Ion to have expertise about. In focusing on a generalized speaking ability, Ion can be thus seen as moving towards something more like ethical knowledge.

The notion of 'fittingness' or 'appropriateness' (*to prepon*) is ambiguous, and it is unclear what exactly Ion has in mind. In particular, it has both a descriptive sense, picking out what one of these figures is likely to say, and a normative sense, picking out what one of these figures ought to say. The former sense is important for poetic composition, which aims at least in part at verisimilitude. The latter sense might be usefully subdivided into two different kinds of norms: what one should say in order to get what one wants (a rhetorical or strategic norm) and what one should say in order to do the right thing (an ethical or epistemic norm). The ambiguity between the descriptive and the normative is crucial to Ion's self-conception, since, as we saw in Section 3.1, it is the implicit inference from Homeric descriptions to Homeric prescriptions that underwrites the very idea that one can gain knowledge from Homer.

Socrates' arguments focus on the normative aspect of appropriateness in the second sense. By specifying for each social role some epistemic role – some knowledge – he forces Ion to acknowledge that the relevant norm is internal to the expertise and thus subject to expert evaluation. Once the speaking norm is shown to be proper to a particular craft, according to the principle of epistemic distinctness, it can no longer be something the rhapsode can claim expertise about. One might get the impression that Socrates has slyly forced Ion back into the craft paradigm, but Socrates' point is presumably that, whenever anyone says something, they say *some thing*, that is, they articulate some content.[45] Ion's social roles are highly general, and it is hard to see what it would be fitting for a woman (or a slave or a leader) to say without specifying some particular situation in which she must speak. The fittingness of those utterances will then have to be evaluated in light of the relevant epistemic standard and by the relevant expert.

Socrates begins with a free, male "leader" (540b6), and this is, I take it, no accident, since rhetoric was advertised as granting men political prominence in

---

[45] Plato is in general skeptical to the idea of generic arts of speaking that are entirely divorced from the content of the speech, and we see this kind of move in *Gorgias* and *Phaedrus*.

their city. However, the leaders he chooses – a navigator on the storm-tossed ship (540b6–8) and a doctor trying to heal a patient (540c1–2) – are not really the kind of leader Ion is envisioning, as doctors and navigators did not enjoy a particularly high social status. The next example is a slave, and Ion is quite willing to affirm that he would know what a slave should say; indeed he must since several slaves speak in Homer. However, he is quickly forced to concede that he is the epistemic inferior of the slave cowherd (540c4–6). For the next example, Socrates remains on the lower end of the social spectrum, and again Ion concedes that he knows less about wool than a woman spinning yarn (540c6–d1). The last example – the general (540d2) – is exactly the kind of free, male leader that Ion thinks he can be on the basis of Homer's poetry. The order of examples primes Ion to jump at the expertise that is both socially honorable and ethically valuable. In short, it is amenable to Ion's self-conception as important that he put himself on par with a general.[46] Socrates also subtly encourages Ion to accept this example by making the general encourage or exhort troops, as opposed to plan troop formations or build ramparts.

Ion claims emphatically that he, qua rhapsode, would know what the general should say: "Yes! That's the sort of thing a rhapsode will know" (540d2–3). Given the principle of epistemic distinctness, Ion must explain and clarify the relation between his apparent expertise in rhapsody and his alleged expertise in generalship. Instead of accepting Socrates' suggestion that he is both a rhapsode and a general, and that it is the latter that explains his knowledge, he claims – bizarrely – that rhapsody and generalship are one and the same expertise (541a2–3)! The suggestion is so absurd that he cannot manage to affirm it coherently: He twice affirms that all "good rhapsodes" are "good generals" (541a3–4; 541a6–b1) but denies, understandably enough, that all good generals are good rhapsodes (541a5–7). Ion comes across as completely ridiculous in this scene, revealing a troubling inability to distinguish between convincingly *appearing like* a figure and really *knowing how* to be that figure. He rejects Socrates' suggestion of dual competence because it would put a gap between his knowledge of Homer and his knowledge of other things, that is, it would not allow him to assert competency in generalship because of his expertise in Homer. When Socrates asks him if he is "the best general in Greece" (541b3–4), Ion replies, "Certainly, Socrates! That, too, I learned from Homer!" (541b4–5). Ion thinks that he has learned a socially valuable and ethically important skill from Homer, and this grounds his sense of his own importance and of the great value of Homer's poetry. In sum, Ion's attempt to attribute a general speaking ability to himself fails because the implication he draws from it – that he is the best general – is absurd on its face. He is not forced by Socrates to withdraw the

---

[46] Cp. Xen. *Symp.* 4.6, quoted in Section 1.

claim, but no reader of the dialogue could fail to see that we are encouraged to dismiss the claim out of hand. Thus, since this last attempt to find content for the rhapsodic expertise fails, it looks like rhapsody is an expertise without content, which is another way of saying that it is not an expertise at all.

Some scholars have seen Ion as gesturing in this section towards a notion of expression, or style, as distinct from content (Murray 540b3 ad loc.). The idea would be that Ion is claiming to know *how* a man, slave, or whatever would and should speak – their tones, gestures, and facial expressions, for example – but not necessarily *what* they would and should say. It does not seem to me that Ion has such an idea in mind, even implicitly, since such stylistic expertise would provide such a thin basis for his claim to be knowledgeable about, and because of, Homer. He would thus only know something very general, namely how to sound and look like a speaking man, woman, or slave. Further, Ion repeatedly claims that he would know what one would say, that is, he points to the *content* of the speech. He may, of course, mean the style or expression *in addition* and may, as I suggest, fail to properly distinguish between seeming like a general and really being one, but it would go too far to attribute a positive view about style to him on this basis.

3.5 Conclusion

The expertise model is a model of poetic reception, that is, it is supposed to tell us something about how the audience is supposed to relate to the poetry. On that model, we treat the poets as epistemic authorities and their poems as sources of wisdom. Thus, the Homer's audience should accept his wisdom and consult his poetry as an authoritative store of knowledge. Those who are experts about Homer have wide-ranging and immediate access to this wisdom and can teach it to their audiences. Thus, rhapsody is a valuable skill, and one can explain rhapsodic success in terms of expertise. In the dialogue, this model is forcefully rejected, Ion is shown not to possess a valuable skill, and the possibility of a rhapsodic expertise is made highly doubtful by the principle of epistemic distinctness. So too is the possibility of a poetic expertise. As we have seen, a core assumption of the expertise model is the content thesis, namely that poetry can teach its audience by transmitting true content to them. Socrates' various lines of questioning all assume that there is some true epistemic content in Homer's poetry to which Ion qua rhapsode is alleged to have special access. The principle of epistemic distinctness makes it hard to explain how the craft of poetry could contain or encompass these other crafts. Further, once Homer's poetry is taken to be about its content, it enters the space of reasons and is subject to evaluation by relevant experts. This at least implicitly calls the epistemic value of poetry into question, by making the poets replaceable by the craftsmen.

What about the content thesis itself? It is not explicitly rejected anywhere in the dialogue, and I do not think that it necessarily must be discarded along with the expertise model. For, while the idea that *there could be* true content in poetry is never explicitly questioned, Socrates puts tremendous pressure on the assumption that *there is* true content in poetry. Further, Socrates questions whether all sorts of passages are good vehicles for content in the first place. It is the assumption of the poet's wisdom that makes the content thesis problematic, for that assumption basically guarantees that there is true content in poetry and that we should find it wherever we find content in Homer. The modality of these claims is crucial here – as I have formulated the content thesis, it just tells us that poetry might transmit true content, not that it necessarily does. What is shown is that any explanation of the presence of true content requires appealing to some expertise other than poetry and any evaluation of content as true requires appealing to some expertise other than rhapsody. The application of the principle of epistemic distinctness shows that, whatever true content about other crafts one finds in Homer's poetry, it cannot be because of poetic expertise that it is there. Thus, the conclusion is not that poetry could not possibly contain true content but that the explanation of how true content got there requires some explanation other than poetic expertise.

The quality of Socrates' arguments has been questioned, both implicitly and explicitly, by those who think that Ion is a mindless pushover. Yet what strategies of resistance might Ion have employed that actually allow him to maintain his sense of his own expertise and importance? First, in several places, Ion might have staked a claim to knowledge about the beauty and aesthetic features of Homer's poetry. He might have judged Homer's poetry as aesthetically superior to Hesiod's. He might have claimed greater competence than doctors, fishermen, and so on regarding the vivid imagery and uses of similes in Homer's verses, and he might have appealed to the aesthetic fittingness of Homer's depictions of speakers, accounting for both descriptive appropriateness and the beauty of the lines spoken. He does not fail to make these suggestions out of stupidity, I submit, but because to restrict his expertise to these narrowly aesthetic matters would severely undercut the value of his expertise and the importance of his interpretive speeches. Second, it has been suggested that Ion might have plausibly claimed expertise on the passages in Homer that feature rhapsodes. Indeed, Socrates implicitly puts this possibility in front of Ion by naming two rhapsodes that Homer himself mentions: Thamyras (533b8), who is blinded for boasting that he would beat the Muses themselves in a contest (*Il.* 2.595–600), and "Phemius of Ithaca" (533c1), who is forced to entertain the suitors (*Od.* 1.153–5) and later begs for his life and is spared by Odysseus (*Od.* 22.330–56). This would satisfy the principle of epistemic distinctness, but it would force Ion to restrict radically the scope of his expertise to the very few passages in Homer where there are rhapsodes. Last, Ion might have foregrounded the ethical dimension of poetry, claiming for Homer, and thus for himself, a more general wisdom about *how to live* rather than knowledge of specialized skills. He might have resisted Socrates' constant pressure to turn the conversation towards craft expertise. This would be consistent with Ion's self-conception, and, as we saw, his last line of defense at least pushes in this direction. However, it would not enable him to escape refutation.[47] For even if we grant that poetic wisdom just is ethical knowledge, the principle of epistemic distinctness still rules out the possibility that Ion has access to Homer's ethical wisdom in virtue of being rhapsode.

4 The Inspiration Model of Poetic Reception

Ion puts himself forward as a counterexample to the expertise model (533c4–8 cp. 532b7–c4), and the inspiration model (533d–536d) is offered as an alternative explanation of the "cause" (532b7) of Ion's singular and exclusive abilities with respect to Homer. Plato connects poets to divine inspiration in several dialogues.[48] The main idea, that the Muse inspires the composing poets, is a traditional one, and Socrates appeals to "the poets themselves" (534a6) as confirming it.[49] The inspiration model is, in many ways, the converse of the expertise model: Whereas the latter explains poetic and rhapsodic success as entirely epistemic and the core of poetry as its content, the inspiration model explains success as entirely aesthetic and the core of poetry as its beauty.[50] Further, because the inspiration model is focused on performance, the audience experience of poetry and its emotional effect – totally absent in the articulation of the expertise model – come to the fore. These differences are also reflected in the style of presentation: metaphors, rhetorical flourish, poetical diction, and signs from god replace straightforward argument and analysis.

In order to understand the content of the inspiration view, we need to explain the metaphors and images. This is challenging not only because it is never obvious

---

[47] Interlocutors claiming a general knowledge of human excellence are not able to escape Socratic refutation: see, e.g., Thrasymachus in *Republic* and Callicles in the *Gorgias*.

[48] The *Phaedrus* contains the most extensive discussion of divine inspiration in general (245a, 249c–245a, 265a–b), but see also *Ap.* 22b–c, *Meno* 99a–e, *Tim.* 71e–72b, and *Laws* 3.682a, 4.719c.

[49] On Democritus as a possible forerunner of this idea, see Stern-Gillet (2004, 179); Tigerstedt (1969, 72–76); Murray (1996, 533e3–5 ad loc.).

[50] The only content mentioned is the claim that poets are inspired (534a–b), but this is merely the exception that proves the rule.

how precisely to unpack a metaphor but also because, on my reading, Socrates is presenting us with a *parody* of a traditional view of poetry,[51] in which certain features of the traditional view are amplified to absurdity. The parody begins by reproducing or imitating the traditional view, while gradually exaggerating it to the point where it seems absurd.[52] This is partly confirmed by the progress of Ion's own reactions, which start out as enthusiastically supportive (535a) and end up with an outright rejection (536d). Though the idiom of this section is rhetorical flourish and parody, we can still identify a core critical argument: The gods are responsible for all poetic and rhapsodic success; thus, no poets or rhapsodes deserve any intellectual credit for their achievements. The parody contributes directly to this argument by providing an exaggerated understanding of what it means for a poet to be inspired. The passage may be usefully broken up into three sections: The first is a speech on the divine inspiration of poets (533d–535a); the second is a dialogue about rhapsodic performance and its emotional effects on the audience (535a–e); and the last brings the general account to bear on Ion's special aptitude in Homer (535e–536d).

4.1 Poetic Inspiration and Passivity

Socrates begins by launching into a long, evocative speech articulating the inspiration model (533d–535a). Given the speech's complex nature as both rhetorically rich and a parody, I will proceed systematically as follows: I will first try to give a clear statement of the core claim, the central analogy, and the main lines of evidence, ignoring for the time being the exaggeration and rhetorical flourish. I will then turn to the parodic features of the speech, showing how Socrates' exaggerations go beyond and ultimately serve to undermine the view.

The core claim of the inspiration model is that a "divine power (*theia dunamis*)" (533d3) is the cause and ultimate source of all good poems and all poetic beauty. The "beautiful poems are neither human nor from humans, but are divine and from the gods" (534e2–4). The magnet analogy is Socrates' vehicle for explaining how inspiration works,[53] and how it links up the poet, the rhapsode, and the audience. Just as the magnet pulls iron rings to it, thus placing the magnetic power in the ring, so too the god inspires the poet, thus putting the power of inspiration in the poet. The poet inspires the rhapsode, who, in turn, inspires audiences. Socrates here compares poetic expertise unfavorably with divine inspiration, making inspiration necessary for being a good poet (533e5–7).[54] The individualized nature of inspiration can easily explain why Ion

[51] Cp. Tigerstedt (1969).   [52] On Plato's use of parody, see Trivigno (2009a, 2012b).

[53] It is unclear whether the magnet analogy is Plato's invention, but the use of the Euripidean name for the stone (533d3–4) gives it at least a poetic resonance. See Murray (1996, ad loc.).

[54] Cp. *Phdr.* 245a, where inspired poets are also compared favorably to those with expertise.

is only concerned with Homer – he is inspired by Homer, but not by the others – and so the account satisfies Ion's request that his exclusive interest in Homer be explained.

Socrates adduces several pieces of evidence in favor of the inspiration model. First, he makes an analogy with other forms of divine inspiration, like inspired prophecy, to bring out features of poetic inspiration – these analogies reveal the extent to which those inspired are psychologically given over to the god and "not in their right mind" (534a2). Second, he appeals to the authority of "the poets themselves" (534a6) who claim, in poetically colored metaphors, to "gather songs from honey-flowing springs in the Muses' glades and gardens" (534b1–2).[55] Third, he makes an abductive argument that the inspiration model provides the best explanation for the poets' actual inability to compose in all poetic genres.[56] Last, he provides the example of the poet Tynnichus, perhaps the world's first one-hit wonder, who composed nothing memorable apart from the "nearly most beautiful lyric poem ever" (534d7–8). This last piece of evidence, Socrates claims, is the "greatest proof" (534d4–5) of the account, a sign from the gods, saying that they, and not the poets, are responsible for such poetry – something Tynnichus himself acknowledged. The upshot is that only some poets are inspired and only some of the time, that is, when they are composing beautiful poetry. The poets are, on this picture, blessed mediators, but not genius creators.

Formulated in this way, the inspiration model can be understood as a seriously intended account of poetic composition in terms of divine inspiration and of the poet as a blessed figure, who composes in a quasi-mystical state of mind. Some have indeed understood this section as laying out Plato's own view, but I think there are clear signals that Socrates' praise of the poet, and by implication the rhapsode, is ironically meant. Socrates goes beyond the traditional idea of poetic inspiration and reformulates the idea in an absurd direction. The account is, in short, a parody. Socrates employs the parodic strategy of amplification, which functions by inhabiting the logic of the target idea and taking it too far, as it were. For the parody to work, the articulation must start out as seemingly serious and maintain contact with the original idea.

The core of Socrates' method consists in amplifying features of being inspired so that it eventually becomes assimilated to being insane. To this end, he uses

---

[55] Consider, e.g., the invocation of the Muses at the beginning of Homer's *Iliad* and Hesiod's *Theogony*.

[56] Some commentators have complained that Socrates' claim that no poet composed well in multiple genres is transparently false, since Plato would have known of Pindar's versatility. Perhaps the point is simply overstated, since no poet mastered *all* genres and most were skilled in a limited number.

three strategies: a linguistic, an argumentative, and an analogical strategy. The linguistic strategy involves assimilating 'inspiration' to 'possession'; as Tigerstedt has argued, there is little evidence of 'possession' language in the tradition on poetic inspiration, such that Plato's use of it here may be reasonably seen as a malicious innovation (1969, 26). The Greek term for inspiration, *entheos*, literally means 'having a god inside,' and, in the case of poetic composition, this might suggest a kind of *joint agency*, whereby the god and the poet are both responsible for the verses and their beauty. Such a conception would allow poets to be both experts and divinely inspired. Socrates' move away from talk of divine 'inspiration,' with its potential for implying joint agency, and towards talk of divine 'possession' (*katechomenos*) is directly supported by the magnet metaphor, since the metal rings are passively 'held' (*echomenos*) by the magnet (536a8–b1). The terms 'inspiration' and 'possession' are used interchangeably in the speech, but they are subtly different, precisely in that possession implies a more passive relation to another who is the single and exclusive agent. Socrates thus understands inspiration as a state in which the god is fully in control and the poet is entirely passive. Poetic composition is, in short, fundamentally irrational, and Socrates goes to great lengths to emphasize the poet's lack of agency.

    The second strategy involves an inference that Socrates makes from the nature of inspiration. Socrates not only denies that the poet, as the first ring in the Muse's chain of inspiration, composes poetry "by means of a craft (*technē*)" (533e6; cp. 534b8, c5) but also denies them mental activity in general. On the inspiration model, epistemic agency of any sort would be a direct hindrance to poetic composition, and Socrates makes being out of one's mind a necessary condition of composing beautiful poetry: "as long as a poet has his intellect in his possession, he will always lack the power to make poetry" (534b6–7). The argument is roughly this: Since poets are inspired when they create beautiful poetry, and inspiration is an entirely passive experience, both knowledge and thinking in general are not possible for the composing poet. This entails that there is no content or knowledge that the poet can claim in virtue of his poetry. Further, it is impossible for a poet to be responsible for his own poetry to the extent that the poetry is any good!

    The last parodic strategy relies on the analogy between the poets' mental state when composing and the mental states of those in two other cases of divine possession: the ritualized ecstatic dancing of Corybantes and Bacchants. The association between divination – for which 'possession' is the appropriate term – and poetry was a traditional part of the poets' self-understanding,[57] but

---

[57] See Murray (1992, 33).

Plato presses the analogy well beyond what the traditional connection would allow. The wild dancing of the Corybantes provides a powerful visual image of those carried away by divine possession. The reference to Bacchic frenzy is even more stark, as the ritual celebrations often involved drinking, nudity, and sex; indeed, the name for the female Dionysian celebrants, the Maenads, literally means 'those who are raving and frantic' (LSJ, s.v. *mainas*). In Euripides' gripping portrayal in the *Bacchae*, the king of Thebes, Pentheus, is literally torn to pieces by the female celebrants, including his mother; he begs for his life, "[b]ut she was foaming at the mouth, and her crazed eyes / rolling with frenzy. She was mad (*ou phronous'*), stark mad, / possessed (*kateichet'*) by Bacchus" (ll. 1122–1124).[58] Given superhuman strength by the god, the women tear him limb from limb. It is in the context of these associations that Socrates provides the strongest description of possession: the poets are "out of their minds (*ouk emphrones*)" (534a1). This analogy thus makes the poets seems insane when composing their poems.[59]

The overall strategy of the speech may be encapsulated in a single sentence: Socrates says, "For a poet is an aery thing, winged and holy, and he is not able to make poetry until he becomes inspired and goes out of his mind and his intellect is no longer in him" (534b3–6). The sentence starts out as apparently high praise with metaphorical richness, but the specifications of being inspired as being out of one's mind and intellectually vacant give an entirely new and deprecating sense to the poet's airiness. Ion does not yet see the implicit criticism in being deemed out of one's mind, but he soon will (536d).

4.2 Emotion and Illusion in Rhapsodic Performance

In this short dialogue (535a–e), Socrates and Ion discuss the emotional effect of the performing rhapsode on his audience. Both rhapsode and audience member, it turns out, are also out of their minds. Ion enthusiastically agrees to Socrates' description of the poets as divinely inspired (535a3–5), and it is easy to see why. The vast majority of the speech offers high praise of the poets as blessed, and the parodic exaggeration is subtle enough to go unnoticed, especially for one whose self-conception is bound up with the reputation of a poet. Because the poets function as "interpreters" of the god, the rhapsodes turn out to be "interpreters of interpreters" since they "interpret what the poets say" (535a5–9). Interpretation is understood here not as a kind of explanation, as in the expertise model, but as a mere transmission.[60] Rhapsodes thus stand in exactly the same passive relation to poets as the poets stand in relation to the god. Since being an

---

[58] Translation by Arrowsmith in Grene and Lattimore (1959).
[59] Cp. Pappas (1989), 281–283.   [60] See Murray (1996, 534e4 ad loc.).

interpreter is always being an interpreter for someone else, this interpretive role for the rhapsode requires some account of what is transported, as it were, to the audience.

Socrates begins his questioning of Ion's effect on the audience as though he admires it, insisting that Ion not "keep any secrets from" him about his state of mind and effect on the audience when he "recite[s] poetry well" (535b1–2). During performances of gripping scenes, both rhapsode and audience are emotionally engaged and psychologically transported. Plato's insight here is that the effect on the audience is parasitic on the emotional engagement of the performer onstage. When Ion performs and recites passages of excitement, fear, and pity, he too feels these emotions. Ion describes these emotions as *real*, detailing the physiological (and thus involuntary) reactions associated with them: his eyes well up with tears, his hairs stand on end, and his heart leaps (535c5–8). Genuinely feeling these emotions when performing Homer is then tied by Socrates to a particular "belief" (535c1), namely that Ion "is present at the actions [he] describes, whether they are in Ithaca or Troy" (535c1–3). This belief is of course false – a kind of illusion – and it is made constitutive of Ion's being inspired or possessed. This justifies Socrates' conclusion that Ion is not "in his right mind" when he performs emotionally jarring scenes (535b7, d1). Socrates takes a detached view of the festival scene, with Ion crying and terrified, even though he is all dressedup, surrounded by an enthralled audience, and nothing is actually happening to him (535d1–5). He seems, in short, like a lunatic.

The relevant passages from Homer are moments of high drama – arguably the climactic scenes of the *Odyssey* and the *Iliad*. The rhapsode's performance has a "stunning effect (*ekplēxēs*)" (535b2) on his spectators,[61] causing in them "the same effects" (535d8–9) he experiences. Thus, the analysis of emotional engagement applies also to the audience. They "are crying and looking terrified and ... filled with amazement" (535e2–3). This must be because they also believe something false, namely that they are present at the events in Ithaca and Troy. This transportation of the audience into the dramatic world of the performer is crucial to the performer's success. Now it is the audience that seems insane. Why should they be crying and terrified when they are comfortably watching a finely dressed performer singing and telling a story and nothing is really happening to anyone? Ion claims to need "to pay attention" (535e4) to make sure that the audience is emotionally engaged, as their enjoyment and thus his monetary compensation depend on this:

---

[61] The term *ekplēxis* picks out sudden, overpowering passions or experiences that shock, amaze, or astound one (LSJ s.v.).

> I look down at [the spectators] every time from up on the rostrum, and they're crying and looking terrified, and as the stories are told they are filled with amazement. You see I must keep my wits and pay close attention to them: if I start them crying, I will laugh as I take their money, but if they laugh, I shall cry at having lost money. (535e1–6)

This moment of self-interested calculation fits awkwardly with the idea that Ion believes that he is in Troy. Indeed, Ion's awareness seems to undermine the inspiration model itself.[62] How can Ion simultaneously be an actively self-aware audience manipulator and a passively inspired conduit of emotion? More broadly, the possibility of emotionally reacting to fictional situations seems to require that one simultaneously believe and not believe them to be real, and this is the heart of the paradox of fiction.

The particular emotions that Socrates highlights in his account of emotional contagion are the tragic emotions of pity and fear.[63] Ion himself divides the kinds of stories he tells into the "pitiful (*eleinon*)" and the "fearful (*phoberon*) or terrifying (*deinon*)" (535c6–7). He further describes his own emotional reactions as involving "tears" and heart-pounding "fear" (535c6, c8). Socrates also picks up this division, describing the rhapsode as performing while he is "weeping" and "afraid" (535d3–4). So too is the audience described as "weeping and looking terrified" (535e2–3). This emotional transference of pity and fear from the performer to the audience is, as Ion makes clear, the criterion of success for his performance. In short, audiences want and expect to be made to feel pity and fear, and they will reward performers who do so. In those cases, it is Ion who gets the last laugh on his bewitched audience by "tak[ing] their money" (535e5–6). If, on the other hand, his performances fail to be gripping, the audience laughs at him. Unable to draw the audience into the world of his illusion, Ion looks like an idiot. In their laughter, the audience sees the situation for what it really is. Indeed, it is this latter perspective that readers are invited to share.

One might object that, in extending the magnet metaphor to the rhapsode and audience, there has been a noticeable and unexplained shift away from divine inspiration and towards emotional engagement, and these seem to be referring to very different phenomenon. What exactly is the connection supposed to be? My suggestion is that, in line with the description of poetic inspiration as a kind of insanity, Socrates looks for signs of inspiration in performers and audiences that make them seem similarly out of their minds, and emotional investment in the world of the poet fits the bill. Further, as I will discuss in Section 5.2, the audience's experience of a performance as beautiful depends on their being

---

[62] See Tigerstedt (1969, 21); Dorter (1973, 72).

[63] The idea that pity and fear are tragic emotions is often attributed to Aristotle, but it is clearly here in the *Ion*, as well as in the *Republic*.

emotionally moved. Unlike the poet's composition, which presumably happens in private, these emotional reactions are publicly available to anyone who has been at a performance. The seer analogy is helpful here: Just as the seer is transported to and can see the world of the future, so too is the rhapsode transported to and living in the world of the poet.[64] Likewise, both performer and audience are transported into and emotionally invested in this poetic world as though it were real. Socrates' core strategy here is again borrowed from comedy: He describes the intense emotional experiences of both rhapsodes and audiences from an external perspective, one that refuses, as it were, to suspend disbelief. From this perspective, the behavior of actors and audiences seems totally bizarre.

4.3 The Inspired Rhapsode

Socrates' final summation of the view (535e7–536d3) now connects the god-poet account to the rhapsode-audience account, and, returning to the magnet metaphor, he finally makes good on the promise to explain Ion's unique interpretive abilities with respect to Homer. In short, the Muse possesses the poet, who possesses the rhapsode, who possesses the audience. Through this chain of inspiration, "the god pulls people's souls wherever he wants" (536a1–3). Whereas the expertise model demanded of the rhapsode a general scope and a unified methodology, the inspiration model individualizes the relation between poet and rhapsode. This final analysis depends on extending the magnet metaphor explicitly to the rhapsodes and audience members and on extending the analysis from performance to interpretation.

The magnet metaphor, when it is initially introduced (533d–e), does not seem to have any comedic or parodic intention. It is focused on the Muse-poet relation and only gestures towards the "chain of other enthusiasts [that are] suspended" from the poet (533e5). When Socrates returns to the metaphor, he describes the spectator as "the last of the rings" and the rhapsode as "the middle ring" (535e7–536a1) in the chain of inspiration. Thus, we have a seemingly neat four-place inspiration relation. Yet Socrates immediately shatters the impression of neatness by extending the metaphor in an absurd and unwieldy manner: "there's an enormous chain of choral dancers and choral trainers and assistant choral trainers hanging off to the sides of the rings that are suspended from the Muse" (536a4–7). It looks like anyone connected to performance in any way becomes connected to the chain of inspiration. The move from choral dancers to choral trainers to assistant choral trainers is surely meant to muddy the waters – while choral dancers are in a position similar to the rhapsode, choral trainers are only

---

[64] For comedic descriptions of the composing poet employing a similar parodic strategy, see Aristoph. *Thesm.* 35–70; *Ach.* 395–417.

indirectly related to performance, and assistant trainers obviously even more so. Plato thus signals that the magnet metaphor is not to be taken very seriously. A more substantial reason that the metaphor is not to be taken seriously is that it quite explicitly makes the gods causally responsible for audience deception, and this cannot be Plato's real view of the matter (cp. *Ap.* 21b, *Rep.* 383a).

Socrates is very keen to establish the negative epistemic conclusion about Ion that follows from his account: Ion is "possessed and held from Homer" (536b5), and, as such, it is "not by craft or knowledge that [he] is able to say what [he] says about Homer" (536c1–2). Few commentators have remarked on the clear move away from performance – Socrates starts with Ion's ability to "recite poetry well (*eu*)" (535b2) – and back to interpretation in the end of this section.[65] Up to this point, Ion's role as 'interpreter of interpreter' has been understood as encompassing only his performances. The lesson of performance is now applied to interpretation. Socrates describes Ion's speeches about Homer as a result of a "divine gift" (536c2, d3) and akin to wild Corybantic dancing. Ion's beautiful thoughts, on this picture, also require that Ion is out of his mind when he speaks. While Ion accepted this characterization when it came to performance, he cannot accept it when it comes to his ability to "praise Homer" (536d6). He explicitly denies being possessed or "crazed" (*mainoenos*) (536d6), and this latter term, though nowhere actually used by Socrates is finally produced as a clear implication of the view. This refusal should be seen as connected to Ion's proclaimed self-awareness when performing. Both are inconsistent with the inspiration model, and they illustrate a deeper dilemma Ion must face between claiming a sort of skill and claiming a connection with the divine. He wants to be both an expert and divinely inspired, and Socrates' exposition shows how the two explanations are mutually exclusive. In any case, Ion has finally understood the critical edge to Socrates' descriptions and to his comparison with inspired seers and ritual ecstatic dancing. He thus rejects the view and begs once again to be allowed to give Socrates a demonstration of his abilities.

4.4 Conclusion

The undeniable presence of exaggeration in Socrates' articulation of the inspiration account has led many simply to reject the whole story out of hand. Consider, for example, Woodruff's judgment that "Plato's story about gods and passive poets is absurd, and he cannot be sincere when he tells it" (1982, 146), or Pappas's contention that the inspiration claim is "as derogatory as any other imputation of insanity" (1989, 381). On the other hand, some scholars have wanted to take the account at least "half seriously" (Stern-Gillet 2004, 178) but without a clear

---

[65] In the initial speech, Socrates only mentions in passing Ion's ability to speak well about Homer (534c1).

method for specifying what exactly is serious and what is not.[66] One prominent suggestion is that the extension of the inspiration account to Ion and rhapsodes is ironic (Murray 1996, 534c1 ad loc.; Greene 1918, 17). This would help explain the move from inspiration to illusion and emotion, and it would be sufficient to undermine the account as a whole, since the magnetic chain analogy falls apart, as Tigerstedt points out (1969, 27). On my reading, there is just too much evidence of exaggeration in the account of the poets themselves to justify reading it as serious, and there is no textual signal that the move from poets to rhapsodes corresponds to a move from serious exposition to comedic exaggeration.

At this point, it might be useful to sketch an alternative reading of the passage, one that takes the account fully seriously, even while acknowledging the obvious signs of manipulation. There are at least two good reasons to consider such a view: First, as mentioned, Plato connects poets to divine inspiration in several places in the corpus. Second, the proposal is placed centrally in the dialogue, in a position parallel to the doctrine of recollection in the *Meno* and the palinode in the *Phaedrus*, where we find a speech with poetical qualities and appeals to divine authority, articulating views that Plato plausibly holds. Instead of following Ficino in taking Socrates' exaggeration as sincerely exuberant celebration, one might explain these features as dialectical. Socrates really believes the inspiration account, and he appeals to poetic authority and to Ion's experience as a performer because these are the kinds of reasons that Ion might accept. A proponent of such a view would have to either accept that Plato really thinks that the gods are the cause of audience deception or, if not, explain, in a principled way, which features of the account are Socrates' exposition and which merely dialectical posturing.

I think that the weight of the evidence is in favor of my reading of the whole inspiration account as a parody of poets' self-understanding that makes poets seems insane and exaggerates poetic passivity to such a degree that it can hardly serve as an explanation of anything. Does this mean that Plato simply rejects the claim that some poets are inspired? Not necessarily. The claim as it is articulated in the *Ion* is different from the way that it is articulated elsewhere, such that it remains possible that there is something true in it even if the current version is wrong. In particular, this version sidelines the content of poetic utterances almost entirely: the poet's 'saying beautiful things' is understood exclusively as 'saying things beautifully,'[67] and there is no content to be had for rhapsodes or audiences. The only belief that is so much as mentioned is a false one. In

---

[66] Cp. Tigerstedt (1969, 26–29).

[67] There is only one formulation that suggests poetic content in the whole of the inspiration account (534b8–c1), but it is surrounded by formulations that emphasize the beauty of how things are said.

Section 7, I will attempt a reconstruction of the inspiration view that puts content at its core. Beauty is very much at the center of the initial articulation of the inspiration account, but it disappears once the account shifts to rhapsodes and audience. What happens to beauty, and how are we to understand what beauty is on the inspiration account? In the next section, I take up the question of beauty directly.

5 The Problem of Beauty

So far, we are left with two unsatisfactory accounts of poetry and rhapsody, two accounts that fail to make sense of Ion's abilities, two accounts that seem to exaggerate to absurdity some important feature of the nature of poetic compos- ition and reception. Both models seem to have a problem with beauty: it is entirely absent on the expertise model and, though initially prominent, it disap- pears on the inspiration model. Shouldn't beauty be central to any account of rhapsody and poetry? In the vase painting of a rhapsode in Figure 3, the inscription reads, "he is beautiful (*kalos*)." How should we understand this claim? These issues force us to ask what makes poetry beautiful and, more broadly, what beauty really is. We can start with the Greek word for 'beautiful,' that is, *kalos*. The standard ancient Greek lexicon lists the three main senses of the adjective *kalos* as the aesthetic ('beautiful'), the utilitarian ('good' or 'of fine quality'), and the moral ('noble' or 'honorable').[68] The adverbial form, *kalōs*, most often indicates the utilitarian sense as 'well' or 'correctly.' In the *Ion*, we find several forms of *kalos*: the ordinary adjective, *kalos*; the adverb, *kalōs*; the superlative, *kallistos*; and the comparative, *kallion*. My purpose here is not to catalogue every instance of the term but to bring the semantic range of *kalos* – and how it relates to other closely related evaluative terms – to bear on the argument of the dialogue. In my discussion so far, I have noted some places where the ambiguity of the Greek word, *kalos* (and its cognate forms), has been important, but I have left the ambiguity intact, as it were.[69] Here, I tackle the problem of beauty head-on, by examining the ambiguous uses of *kalos* in order to map out its semantic range, clarify the challenge posed by the ambiguities of beauty, and articulate what true or real beauty might entail on a Platonic picture.

5.1 Ion's Understanding of *kalos*

At the beginning of the dialogue, Ion is praised by Socrates because his craft requires him to "appear as beautiful as [he] can (*hōs kallistoi phainetai*)" (530b7–8)

---

[68] See LSJ, s.v. *kalos*.
[69] Woodruff's translation does an excellent job of preserving the ambiguity of *kalos*. See also Dorter (1973, 75–76). On the wide variety of things that can be described as *kalos*, see *Hip. Ma.*; *Symp.* 210a–e.

and because, to complete the interpretative task of the rhapsode "beautifully (*kalōs*)" (530c5), he needs to know the thought of Homer. Already we see the semantic range of *kalos* come into play, for the first instance is clearly and exclusively aesthetic in nature, since it concerns the clothing and outward appearance of the rhapsode, whereas the second instance is less clear. It could be taken in the utilitarian sense ('well'), since a condition (knowing Homer's thought) is made instrumental to the correct performance of a task (interpreting Homer for the audience). The implied norm or standard would be getting it right, or accurately relating what Homer thought. Alternatively, it could be taken in a more aesthetic sense: When it comes to an interpretation of Homer delivered to an audience, what makes it beautiful is the elegance of his speech. The speech would be pleasing to hear, with clever turns of phrase, and the implied norm would not be getting it right but impressing the audience. How we understand this is connected to how we understand another evaluative term, *agathos*, or 'good,' whose sense overlaps with that of *kalos*, for Socrates has made all this necessary for being "a good (*agathos*) rhapsode" (530c2). What, then, is a good rhapsode? What does a rhapsode do well?

Ion seems to endorse an aestheticizing account of what makes for a good rhapsode. He claims that he is able to "speak more beautifully (*kallista*) about Homer than anyone" (530c8–9). He elaborates on this by saying that no one else "is

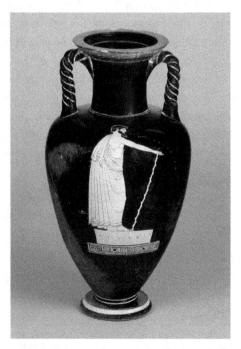

Figure 3 Rhapsode with staff © The Trustees of the British Museum.

able to express as many beautiful thoughts (*pollas kai kalas dianoias*) about Homer" as he can (520c9–d3). This is a clear linguistic signal that Ion is claiming that his speeches are beautiful as in 'impressively delivered,' and not – at least not necessarily – in terms of 'accurately relating Homer's thought.' Ion wants to impress Socrates with "how well (*eu*) [he has] adorned (*kekosmēka*) Homer" (530d6–7). The term Ion uses here, *kosmeō*, to 'adorn' or 'embellish' (LSJ s.v.) is the etymological ancestor of the English word, 'cosmetics.' The idea is that Ion beautifies and praises Homer when he speaks about him, and the very last line of the dialogue describes Ion as a "singer of Homer's praises" (542b4; cp. 536d3, 536d6). After Socrates tries to get Ion to connect rhapsodic interpretation to the epistemic content of Homer's thought and the value of Homer's thought to its truth or correctness, Ion still insists on his aesthetic formulation: "I speak about Homer more beautifully (*kallist'*) than anybody else and I have lots to say; and everyone else says I do it well (*eu*)" (533c5–7). Ion appeals to the testimony of other people to validate his competence, but, instead of bringing in experts, as Socrates had done, he brings in audiences. To such people, he is able to appear to speak beautifully. This picks up on Socrates' initial claim that Ion gets to "appear" as beautiful as he can. If all there is to speaking beautifully about Homer is appearing to many people to speak beautifully about Homer, then Ion's claim stands.

We see this aestheticizing understanding of good speaking when Ion comments on Socrates' abilities. When Socrates asks Ion if he should explain what it means to say that each craft has a unified methodology, Ion replies: "Oh lord yes, Socrates, I love to hear you wise men speak!" (532d4–5). Ion thinks that Socrates is, like him, a performer, whose 'wisdom' can be demonstrated by enthralling an audience. He thinks the context is that of display speeches, or *epideixeis*, where cleverness and linguistic virtuosity are the norms of success. Ion is very keen "to give a demonstration (*epideixai*)" of his own ability to give speeches about Homer (530d5). Later, when Ion finally sees the implications of the inspiration model, he says:

> You're a good speaker (*eu legeis*), Socrates. Still, I would be amazed if you could speak well enough to convince me that I am possessed or crazed when I praise Homer. I don't believe you'd think so if you heard me speaking on Homer. (536d4–7)

Ion is duly impressed by Socrates' speaking abilities, but this by no means entails that he will change his mind about himself.[70] Instead, Ion really wants to get his turn, as it were, and be able to show off his own abilities. That, he thinks,

---

[70] Ion seems to commit himself implicitly to a norm of persuasion, but one prominent kind of display speech attempted to convince its audience of an apparently hopeless case: see, e.g., Gorgias' *Encomium to Helen*.

will surely convince Socrates that he has a valuable skill, for he assumes that Socrates will be just as impressed as everyone else.

At the very end of the dialogue, Socrates chastises Ion repeatedly for failing to "give a demonstration (*epideixein*)" (541e4, e5, 542a1, a3) of his abilities and knowledge of Homer. This may seem wildly unfair of Socrates. It was Socrates who initially asked for a demonstration only to demur. Yet there is a significant gap between what Ion understands Socrates to be requesting and what Socrates really wants demonstrated. An *epideixis* involves a displaying of oneself (LSJ s.v.), and Ion wants to give a demonstration in the sense of a display speech of his speech-making virtuosity in praising Homer, whereas Socrates wants one in the sense of proof or evidence of who Ion really is.[71] By making Homer seem beautiful and impressive, Ion wants to display himself as beautiful and impressive. Socrates, on the other hand, wants a demonstration of what Ion's "craft and expertise" consist in (541e2), specifying the nature of his alleged expertise and thus revealing who he really is.[72]

Socrates offers Ion a final choice: either he has expertise about Homer and is unjust for refusing to explain it or he is divine but has no expertise: "How do you want us to think of you – as an unjust *man* or as someone *divine*?" (542a6–7). Ion's response is telling: "it is much more beautiful (*kallion*) to be thought (*nomizesthai*) divine" (542b1–2). Ion first of all chooses the option that best reflects his high opinion of himself. Second, he simply accepts that the choice is framed as between two ways of *being thought of by others*; in short, he embraces the idea that his concern is mainly with reputation or appearance. Third, Ion's use of *kallion* seems to be in line with his generally aesthetic understanding – Woodruff 's "lovelier" is a good translation – but in this case it is used in deciding who he is as a human being. Thus, it is a use that inevitably slides over into the ethical or moral sense, overlapping with something like "more noble"; and here we see the real problem with an aestheticizing understanding of *kalos*, namely that it can lead one to think that what makes a life good and noble just is appearing beautiful or noble to others. This is connected to Ion's mistakenly thinking that he knows how to be a general because he convincingly appears to be one to his audience. This line of thinking can be a source of foolish self-ignorance, as I will demonstrate in Section 6.

5.2 The Deceptiveness of Beauty

Beauty is centrally important to the inspiration model. One sees this, first and foremost, in Socrates' manner of expression, which is poetic and elaborate,

---

[71] See LSV s.v. *epideiknumi*.
[72] Woolf (1997) draws a very tight connection between selfhood and knowledge.

articulating a beautiful speech that captivates Ion: "it touches his soul" (535a3–4). Beauty is mentioned explicitly in connection with Homer's verses, and variants of *kalos* occur repeatedly in Socrates' opening account of the inspiration model: eight times in just over a single Stephanus page, by far the greatest concentration of *kalos*-terms in the dialogue. There is surprisingly, however, no talk of beauty in the rest of the inspiration account. I will first examine the significance of beauty in the initial speech and then argue that beauty 'disappears' because it is made the vehicle for audience deception.

Socrates makes inspiration a necessary condition for poets to "utter all those beautiful poems (*panta tauta ta kala . . . poiēmata*)" (533e7–8) and to "compose those beautiful verses (*ta kala melē tauta*)" (534a2). Socrates restricts inspir-ation and the composition of beautiful poetry to "good (*agathoi*)" poets (533e6, e9). The poet's ability "to say many beautiful things (*polla . . . kai kala*)" (534b8) is a divine gift that is specialized by genre, since "each is able to compose beautifully (*kalōs*) only that genre for which the Muse has aroused him" (534c2–3). Indeed, Socrates goes even further, saying that it is the gods' intention in inspiring poets that listeners should understand that the poets "are not the ones who speak those verses of great value (*aixa pollou*)" (534d2–3) and that "those beautiful poems (*ta kala tauta poēmata*)" (534e3) are the work of the gods themselves. The otherwise unremarkable Tynnichus produced "nearly the most beautiful (*kalliston*) lyric poem there is" (534d7–8); and "the god intentionally sang the most beautiful (*kalliston*) lyric poem through the most worthless (*phaulotatou*) poet" (534e6–535a1) to prove this point. These *kalos*-terms, including the adverbial cases, are used exclusively in their aesthetic sense. To speak beautifully and to compose beautifully are used interchange-ably, indicating the production of beautiful poems.

Given this emphasis on the divinely inspired beauty of poetry, one might expect beauty to shine through such that audiences may directly experience it. Yet when Socrates discusses rhapsodic performance and audience experience, beauty vanishes.[73] What we get instead is emotional engagement and deception, and it is left highly unclear why this is caused by divinely inspired beauty. The "stunning effect" (535b2) produced by Ion's performances is one that strongly engages audience emotions: when they "weep, look terrified . . . and are astounded by the story being told" (535e2–3), they most of all enjoy the performance. The experience of the captivated audience depends on the illusion that they are at the events taking place and that those events are real. Is the connection between beauty, on the one hand, and emotion-illusion, on the other,

---

[73] One might be tempted to supply the notion of 'aesthetic pleasure.' While Plato is keenly aware of beauty's ability to cause pleasure (see e.g. *Phdr.* 251d, *Symp.* 206d), he does not think that there is a *sui generis* aesthetic pleasure disconnected from value and emotion.

merely accidental? I think not. First, the experience of beauty seems likely to cause an intense emotional reaction in its audience, so making emotional engagement a sign of the experience of beauty does not seem unreasonable. Second, it is plausible to suppose that the experience of beauty will captivate and enthrall its audience, drawing them into the poem's world. Thus, understanding the experience of beauty as involving submission to an illusion certainly makes sense. Indeed, those who do not submit to the illusion will simply laugh at it, not experiencing it as beautiful at all (535e).[74]

If I am right, then the experience of poetic beauty is, in the inspiration account, bound up with emotion and deception.[75] Plato does not here give any more information on how the causal, psychological mechanisms are supposed to work.[76] This is not surprising, given that the overall purpose of the articulation of the inspiration model is to exaggerate to absurdity the poetic idea of divine inspiration. However, it is worth trying to connect the dangers associated with Ion's aestheticizing understanding of *kalos* (from Section 5.1) to the idea that poetic beauty causes emotion and illusion. By captivating an audience and pulling them into the world of Homer, Ion might cause the audience to make the same kind of mistake he does about the sufficiency of *appearing* beautiful to being noble or living a good life.[77] Indeed, Ion wants the audience to think that he is beautiful on the basis of his appearing so in his performances, and he wants them to think that Homer is beautiful because of Ion's enthralling performances. Further, the audience might, in the grip of the poetic illusion, accept that characters within Homer's poetry who *appear* to be beautiful or noble really *are* good. In fact, Ion's claim to be the best general implicitly relies on this idea – his claim to be the best general only makes sense if Homer's generals really are good. In these cases, Plato would insist that the audience is making a grave mistake. Thus, the beautiful deceptions experienced by the audience are plausibly morally harmful.

5.3 Beauty and Correctness

In the expertise model, *kalos* is understood in a way that basically excludes its aesthetic sense. In one way, beauty disappears; in another, it reemerges in its connection to truth. As I will show, the *kalos*-terms we find in the passages that

---

[74] Cp. *Rep.* 601a–b, where the superficial beauty of poetry is stripped away to reveal the shortcomings of its content.

[75] Woodruff claims that Socrates simply "views mere beauty as a deception" (1982, 141). As I argue in Section 5.4, this is true in the inspiration account, but it is not Plato's final word on the matter.

[76] See *Rep.* 10 for such an account.

[77] Cp. the lovers of sights in the *Republic* (475d–476c), who are satisfied with the mere appearance of beauty (cp. 505d).

elaborate this model suggesting understanding Ion's ability to "say many beautiful things" and "speak beautifully" about Homer as an ability to say many correct or accurate things about the crafts that Homer depicts. As in the account of the inspiration model, *kalos*-terms are initially prominent but then disappear; they are replaced by other evaluative terminology that Socrates uses in order to spell out how rhapsodes do interpretive work "well." Beauty is here understood in a veridical way, as correctness or accuracy. To speak or act beautifully, then, is not a question of one's appearance or aesthetic qualities but of one's relation to the truth. In general, this veridical understanding of beauty is positive; however, in at least two passages, we may begin to wonder if it is missing something important.

Ion is first asked whether he would "explain better (*kallion*)" (531a7) Homeric passages on divination when they agree with Hesiodic passages. Here the comparative form of *kalos* must be taken to something like 'more accurately,' since the premise of the question is that the two authors agree on the content, that is, on how to practice divination. This lays the groundwork for Ion to admit that "one of the good (*agathōn*) diviners" would "explain better (*kallion*)" than Ion passages in which Homer and Hesiod both agree and disagree (531b5–6). The emphasis here is on the quality of the *explanation*, which is enabled by the epistemic status of the agent, and not on its aesthetic features. Ion's position is that, whenever there is a disagreement between Homer and other poets, regardless of subject, those others are much "worse (*kakion*)" and Homer is decidedly "better (*ameinon*)" (531d8–11). Socrates rejects such an ad hoc and unsubstantiated declaration by arguing that the comparative *evaluation* of two speakers also depends on the agent's knowledge. On this picture, to *explain* where two people disagree involves the ability to *evaluate* which one is right and which wrong.

Socrates adduces several examples to determine what makes for an "adequate judge (*kritēn hikanon*)" (532b5), that is, one who is well placed to explain and evaluate such cases. It is, in all cases, the same person, the one with knowledge. We are told, in the example of arithmetic, that the one with knowledge will be able to identify the one who "speaks best (*arista*)" (531d13) and to distinguish between the one "speaking well (*eu*)" and those "speaking badly (*kakōs*)" (531e1–2). Regarding health, the doctor will identify the one who speaks "best (*arista*)" (531e5, e6, e7), as well as those speaking "worse (*kakion*)" (531e7). The general lesson is that the one with knowledge in any field is always able to differentiate between those speaking "well (*eu*)" and those speaking "badly (*kakōs*)" (532a1, a2). The result is that Ion, if he really knows and can explain why Homer speaks "well (*eu*)," must also know and be able to explain why those others, including Hesiod, are "worse (*cheiron*)" (532a7, a8–b1). So far, the picture of what it means for Ion to speak *kalōs* about Homer and evaluate Homer as speaking *kalōs* is straightforward: one speaks *kalōs* when one speaks knowledgeably and only one with knowledge in the relevant field is in a position to explain and evaluate *kalōs* what any given speaker has said.

Socrates then turns to critics of the fine arts, and he departs from cases of an expert speaker evaluating other speakers. This complicates matters. When it comes to painters, Ion admits that there are and have been "good and bad (*agathoi kai phauloi*)" (532e6–7) painters and that some critics are "clever (*deinos*) at showing" what is "well (*eu*) painted and not" (532e8–9). So too for sculpture: the one who is "clever (*deinos*) at explaining" (533b2) why one sculptor's works are "well (*eu*) made" (533b3) is able to explain the same for all the others. The same general point holds for those who are "clever (*deinos*) at explaining" (533b8) when something is done "well (*eu*)" (533c3) in various artistic disciplines like flute-playing, cithara-playing, singing to the cithara, and rhapsodizing. These examples potentially raise some problems for the understanding of beauty as accuracy or correctness. It is not at all clear that painting, sculpture, and music have the same kind of content as mathematics and medicine, such that one could evaluate their products as accurate or correct.[78] Indeed, it may seem natural to make aesthetic beauty the condition of well-made artistic products. The identification of being *kalōs* with accuracy or correctness seems thus subtly undermined by turning to the fine arts. These examples show that the exclusion of the aesthetic sense of beauty may be problematic in some domains.

When Socrates returns to the expertise model, he continues to use *kalos*-terms in the utilitarian sense. In the discussion of Ion's purported ability to know what is fitting for any sort of person to say, Socrates gets Ion to admit that a navigator and a doctor would know "better (*kallion*)" (540b7, c2) than a rhapsode what to say in a storm and to a sick man. However, in discussing the Homeric passages, Socrates really puts pressure on the understanding of beauty as correctness by repeatedly pairing *kalōs* with *orthōs*, 'correctly.' Socrates first asks whether a doctor or a charioteer would "know better (*ameinon*)" whether or not Homer "speaks correctly (*orthōs*)" (537c1–2) in the passage. This seems straightforward enough, and Ion agrees that a charioteer would know better. A bit later, Socrates asks whether the charioteer would "know better (*kallion*)" than a rhapsode whether Homer "speaks beautifully (*kalōs*)" (538b2) about charioteering. These questions, and the terms *kalōs* and

---

[78] Plato's view in the *Republic* and *Laws* does allow for correctness conditions for such arts, but such conditions are simultaneously aesthetic and indexed to audience effect and thus quite different from the kind of correctness we find in the expertise model. See, e.g., Moss (2012) and my discussion in this section.

orthōs, are taken to be equivalent. Socrates' subtle shift in formulation from *orthōs-ameinon* to *kalōs-kallion* is interesting, since an aesthetic understanding of *kalōs* might have generated a different response. In the next example, Socrates asks whether a doctor or a rhapsode "would diagnose beautifully (*kalōs*)" whether or not "Homer speaks correctly (*orthōs*)" (538c4–5) in the passage. This is a surprising reversal, since one expects a diagnosis to be correct and poetry to be beautiful. Again, it seems like Plato subtly hints at the aesthetic qualities of the verses. In the third passage, Ion is asked whether a rhapsode or a fisherman would be in a position to "judge" whether Homer "speaks beautifully (*kalōs*) or not" (538d4–5) in the simile between a god and a fishing hook descending to the sea floor. In this case, the aesthetic sense of *kalōs* is hard to ignore. Homer was well known for his elaborate similes,[79] and it would not have been unreasonable for Ion to claim competency regarding the simile and its beauty.

Most importantly for my larger task in Section 5, these passages raise questions regarding how exactly we are to understand *kalos*. On the one hand, we have a positive, veridical role for *kalos* as accurate or correct. This is a clear improvement over the deceptive and epistemically dangerous notion we found on the inspiration model. Yet this positive notion of *kalos* seems highly limited to what is correct as determined by craft experts – as descriptively true but without aesthetic qualities at all – but, we have seen, these passages seem to call attention to the fact that the aesthetic aspect is missing. Is Plato pushing us towards a positive notion of *kalos* that goes beyond the merely technically correct and can incorporate the aesthetic sense of beauty? To this question, I now turn.

5.4 True Beauty

In this section, I will try to think with and beyond the text of the *Ion* in order to see whether there is any logical space for these two poles of *kalos* – the aesthetic and veridical – to be contained in the same notion.[80] It might be that they simply exclude one another, since, as we have seen, the inspiration model seems to connect the aesthetic aspect of beauty inevitably to deception and illusion, and the veridical understanding of beauty seems to make the aesthetic notion entirely irrelevant. On the other hand, this mutual exclusion might just be incidental features of the particular way those notions are fleshed out in the respective accounts and not, at least not necessarily, intended by Plato to

---

[79] See Arist., *Rhet.* 3.11.

[80] Cp. Dorter (1973, 75–76). He also thinks the dialogue gestures towards a deeper sense of beauty, but his view that poetry can directly imitate the divine strikes me as going too far.

exclude each other in principle. Further, I have tried to show some ways in which the text indicates some unease with the exclusive uses of these notions, and this signals that readers might want to begin to ask questions along these lines. The task of this section is primarily conceptual, that is, aimed at sketching ways of unifying the two approaches to understanding *kalos* that are consistent with what is claimed in the *Ion*. Plato discusses beauty directly in other dialogues like *Hippias Major*, *Symposium*, and *Republic*, and I will be drawing on those reflections in order to think through the conceptual possibilities. I think that there are at least three ways of thinking about how one might understand what we might call 'true beauty.'

The first is *incidental*: A verse containing true content about some topic, medicine for example, might also be beautiful. Since the content is, by assumption, entirely divorced from the aesthetic features of the verse, this is surely possible. For example, Hippias claims to have a speech that is "really beautifully constructed" (*Hip. Ma.* 286a5–6), and its aesthetic beauty certainly does not rule out true content. That said, it may be that these two considerations pull in different directions in the case of poetry. Making the lines more beautiful might cause one to sacrifice the content and making the content more accurate might cause one to sacrifice some beauty, but this is a pragmatic and not a principled consideration. Further, given the kinds of Homeric passages that are adduced in the *Ion* as potentially providing epistemic content, there is no reason to assume that they need to be intensely emotional or captivating.

The second way is *instrumental*: A beautiful and captivating poem may be the *means* by which poetry confers true content to its audience. We can imagine two kinds of cases here. First, true content may be expressed poetically using rhythms and harmonies that captivate the audience. The poem's aesthetic features may thus enable audience reception of its content. Second, a captivating scene may draw one into the illusion that one is there witnessing the events and this illusion enables the audience member to grasp some true content. In this case, the content and the illusion would have to be operating on different levels. Under the influence of that illusion, one might be more open to the content that is being presented. For example, in the *Republic* and the *Laws*, the youth are to act out scenes of virtuous agency in order to train them to become good. Such performances require the kind of illusion that Ion undergoes. The relevant content might be some claim that is made within the scene, or the scene itself illustrates some more general truth. For example, the idea that virtue makes one happy could be presented in this way.

The third way is *fundamental*: The beauty of the subject may be part of the true content being conveyed. On this picture, the beauty of the portrayal is essential to conveying true content, such that failure to convey the beauty would

be a failure of content. This forces one to consider what *really is* beautiful or
kalos. In the *Symposium*, bodies, souls, laws, forms of knowledge, and the form
of beauty itself are increasingly perfect and truer instantiations of beauty
(210a–211d).[81] Poetry could present what really is beautiful as beautiful,
employing a kind of truth standard for beauty (cp. *Laws* 667c–668a). For
Plato, the beauty of a soul, for example, is its *virtue* or moral goodness.[82] The
best (*aristos*) human being is the one with virtue (*aretê*). Virtuous agency is the
primary subject matter for poetry in the educational programs of the *Republic*
and *Laws*. Presenting an accurate depiction of virtuous agency as beautiful
can be a way to capture the *nobility* of the virtuous agent, that is, being *kalos* in
the moral sense. This is no illusion, since the virtuous agent really is beautiful
and will always appear so to those with knowledge. Indeed, the presentation
encourages the audience to take up the latter's truth-tracking perspective. In the
Republic, the true depiction of virtuous agency also *determines* the appropriate
rhythms and harmonies such that these too would cohere with the agent's
character and could, in a sense, also be true (400d). Further, the captivating
and accurate representation would be emotionally engaging, but in this case the
emotional response caused by the scene would also be accurate; responding
with awe and admiration would properly reflect the value of a virtuous agent's
actions (cp. *Rep.* 401e; *Laws* 653a–c). Such poetry could lead the audience to
love of the form of beauty itself (*Rep.* 403c; *Laws* 654c–d).[83]

To sum up, there is a merely aesthetic sense of beauty that is connected to
audience deception, and Ion himself embodies the dangers of taking one's self-
understanding as a function of the extent to which one appears beautiful to an
audience. The veridical sense of beauty as correctness connects beauty to truth,
but in a way that seems limited to technical matters, reducing poetry to a vehicle
for craft-knowledge. The limitations of these two conceptions of *kalos* suggest
trying to find a way to understand how *kalos* could incorporate both aesthetic
and veridical beauty. Of the three paths to unity – the incidental, the instrumental, and the fundamental – only the last one provides a genuine unity centered on
the moral sense of *kalos*, and it is plausibly in line with Plato's larger ethical and
metaphysical commitments.[84] It should be noted that we could never, by any of
these means, attain *knowledge*. Such true content could at best transmit true
opinions to its audience and give them practice in the right emotional responses.

---

[81] I doubt that the form of beauty can be directly represented in poetry, as opposed to being
represented via its instantiations, but I leave the question open here.

[82] On the broader connection between beauty and goodness in Plato as we find it in the *Republic*
(e.g. at 452e and 517c), see Lear (2006, 107–109).

[83] See Lear (2006).

[84] Cp. Moss's argument for a unified conception of *kalon* in the *Laws* (2012, 206–209).

6 The Foolishness of Ion

In this section, I return to the theme of Ion's character. Here, I argue, first, that Ion possesses the basic features of a comedic imposter. I then show how Socrates, as ironist, exposes Ion as an imposter: He repeatedly draws Ion into boasting with ironic praise of the rhapsodes' abilities only to show him repeatedly that he lacks the knowledge that he claims to have. Socrates' purpose in drawing Ion out and deceiving him in this way is to educate and improve him, not just to expose and mock him. Finally, I connect Ion's foolishness with self-ignorance and argue that Plato wants to diagnose the nature and source of Ion's self-ignorance. Ion believes both that he really can do the things that he successfully persuades audiences that he can do and that Homer can be consistently relied on as a source of wisdom. These beliefs make him into a fool. Readers of the dialogue laugh at Ion because of his self-ignorance, but we also need to pay attention to our own relationship to poetry to avoid making the same mistake. This is an important lesson because the idea that one could become wise by knowing the work of Homer was widespread in Plato's time, not merely the idle thoughts of a stupid rhapsode.

6.1 Ion As a Comedic Imposter

Plato portrays Ion as a comedic imposter, or *alazōn*, a stock figure from ancient Greek Comedy, who is "an impudent and absurd pretender" who attempts to lay claim to what he does not deserve.[85] In Aristophanes' comedies, these figures are either well-known Athenians, like Socrates, Euripides, or Cleon, or professional types, like doctors, cooks, or politicians. The intellectual version of the imposter, of which Socrates in the *Clouds* is a prime example, has three basic features:

1. He professes to have expertise.
2. He exploits this alleged expertise for money, status, or power.
3. He is exposed as useless or a fraud.

An imposter usually attempts to get some benefit from the comic hero, who deals with him in an ironic way, pretending to take him seriously, before sending him away empty-handed, often with a beating to boot! In an instructive imposter scene in the *Birds*, Peisetairos is sacrificing to the gods and about to have a celebratory feast, when a string of imposters turn up, all wanting to take part (862–1057). The priest, the poet, the oracle monger, Meton (a famous

---

[85] Cornford (1961, 122). On the imposter, see Cornford (1961, 115–146); MacDowell (1990). Cp. pseudo-Pl. *Def.* 416a10–11; Theophr. *Char.* 23. In Aristotle, the imposter is defined together with, and in opposition to, the ironist: *EN* 1108a20–22; *EN* 1127a13–b32; *EE* 1221a24–25.

mathematician), the inspector, and the decree seller are all treated with irony
and contempt and sent away; most are beaten as well. The core textual support
for this Platonic use of comedy comes from two passages: First, in the *Philebus*,
'the laughable,' *to geloion*, is defined as a particular character flaw, namely self-
ignorance, especially in relation to virtue and wisdom (48e). Second, the
comedic exposure of the imposter corresponds to Socrates' practice of exposing
the self-ignorance of poets, politicians, and craftsmen in the *Apology* (21a–23b).

Ion clearly possesses the three characteristics of the comedic imposter.[86]
First, Ion lays claims to knowledge repeatedly in the dialogue, both on his
own and by endorsing Socrates' praise, and he repeatedly boasts about his own
abilities. It will be useful to briefly catalogue his knowledge-claims and boasts.
First and foremost, Ion repeatedly claims to possess an expertise. Ion claims to
know both Homer's "verses," in that he has memorized Homer's poetry, and
his "thought," in that he understand what Homer's poetry means (530b10–c1).
He claims to know how to "speak beautifully about Homer" better than any
rhapsode that has ever lived (530c7–d3, 533c5–7, 541b2–3). Ion also claims to
know all of the subjects of Homer's poetry (531a–d, 536e, 539e), to be able to
"explain" Homer's poetry (531a7), and to be able to evaluate Homer's treatment
of all subjects as "better" than other poets (531d10–11). Ion claims that he
"knows (*gnōsetai*)" (540b2), qua rhapsode, "what's fitting to say" (540b3) for
men, women, slaves, freemen, followers, and leaders. In particular, and most
extravagantly, he claims to "know (*gnoiēn*) what a general should say" (540d5;
cp. 540d1–3), to possess the expertise of the general (540e7–9, 541a1–3,
541a3–4), and to be "the best general in Greece" (541b3–4). In a central
passage, Ion also claims self-knowledge: "But this I know about myself
(*emautōi sunoida*): I speak about Homer more beautifully than anybody else
and I have lots to say; and everyone says I do it well" (533c5–7; cp. 532b8–c4).

Second, Ion is clearly interested in reaping the rewards of his alleged expertise in Homer and repeatedly points to his festival victories, his reputation, and
the financial gain his expertise has garnered him. Ion boasts about his festival
victory in Epidaurus and claims to deserve "to be crowned by the Sons of
Homer with a golden crown" (530d6–8). Winners of such contests were
rewarded with either money or valuable golden crowns, so his claim is another
way of saying that he is the best Homeric rhapsode, who should be compensated
accordingly. As evidence for his ability to speak beautifully about Homer,
Ion appeals to his reputation, what "everyone says" about him (533c6–7). When
performing scenes, Ion has his mind on the "money" he will take from the

---

[86] In Trivigno (2012a), I focused on the presentation of Ion as an imposter in the final scene. Here
I give a fuller account of his character.

audience if he gets them to cry (535e1–6). For Ion, captivating his audience is how he wins prizes and is rewarded financially. In making Homer's poetry seem beautiful, he himself seems beautiful. Ion uses his alleged expertise, in short, in order to gain money and status and to appear impressive and important, that is, *kalos*, to his audience.

The last feature is that the imposter's alleged expertise is exposed as useless or fraudulent by the ironist. I think it is fairly obvious that Socrates ironically praises Ion, induces and encourages many of Ion's knowledge-claims, and subsequently exposes his knowledge as useless. However, the nature and significance of Socratic irony is a highly controversial issue, and, in the next subsection, I will try to articulate how exactly Socrates does these things in his role as ironist.

6.2 Socratic Irony

There is no scholarly consensus as to how to understand Socratic irony,[87] and thus my way of construing how it functions in the *Ion* is inevitably controversial. In particular, while most scholars claim that Socratic irony is entirely distinct from the ancient notion of *eirōneia* and thus only distantly related to the comedic figure of the *eirōn*,[88] I claim that Plato's presentation of Socrates as ironist is squarely in line with this usage and literary tradition. In general, the comedic figure of the ironist is one who feigns ignorance or stupidity, along with friendliness or solicitousness, in relation to some other figure, and thereby exposing that figure as ludicrous to the drama's audience.[89] On this view of irony, then, the core of irony consists in the established relationship to the imposter, and its core expression comes in Socrates' *ironic praise*, and not in his denial of wisdom as Vlastos famously claims.[90] The beating that the imposter gets from Socrates is an argumentative beating that often leaves the imposter confused and speechless – in *aporia* – ideally in doubt about his own abilities. This is, from a Socratic perspective, genuine moral improvement. In the *Ion*, Socrates exposes Ion's lack of self-knowledge, by ironically submitting to Ion's authority through praise and then by undermining that authority through Ion's failed attempts to explain himself. It is crucial that the irony is evident to

---

[87] Important recent work on Socratic irony include Vlastos (1991); Vasiliou (1999); Lane (2006); Lear (2006); Wolfsdorf (2007); and Ferrari (2008).

[88] See, e.g., Vlastos (1991); Vasiliou (1999); Lane (2006). Scholars resist this identification for roughly two reasons: some are unwilling to attribute deception to Socrates, whereas others start with a conception of irony that excludes deception.

[89] Cornford (1961, 119–122, 139–140); Diggle (2004). Cp. Pl. *Symp.* 216e4–5; *Rep.* 1.336e2–337a7; Arist. [*Rh. Al.*] 21; and Theophr. *Char.* 1. See Note 85.

[90] See Nightingale (1995), who notes that discussions of Socratic irony often focus exclusively on Socrates' denial of wisdom.

the reader but invisible to the imposter, who is deceived.[91] Socrates also repeatedly signals the double edge of his praise by his consistent use of "clever," or *deinos*, to describe Ion's epistemic state. In what follows, I will examine four scenes of Socratic irony, in order to show how they relate to one another and how the pattern of ironic praise is aimed at exposing Ion's self-ignorance. Further, I argue that Socrates uses irony to clarify the structure of Ion's knowledge-claims, and this aspect of ironic praise has not been noticed before.

At the beginning of the *Ion*, Socrates sets up the dramatic interplay between himself and Ion by praising him. Socrates repeats three times that he envies Ion (530b5, c1, c6). The purpose of this insistence is to establish Socrates as an epistemic inferior to Ion, insofar as Ion possesses an enviable expertise, rhapsody, and to articulate the basis for this praise. Ion is enviable because he possesses a particular "craft" (530b6) and Socrates does not. Socrates elaborates two aspects of Ion's expertise that make it worthy of praise: (1) he appears beautiful (530b7–8) and (2) he spends time with the poets (530b8–9). Thus, the irony here is already operating on multiple levels, since Socrates praises Ion for having expertise, and that expertise is praised for entailing a beautiful appearance and intimate familiarity with poets. Socrates is disingenuous at both levels, but the irony here is logically structured such that the twofold praise of the rhapsodic expertise is subordinate to (and a continuation of) the praise of Ion. In addition, the second praiseworthy feature of rhapsody is further specified as (2a) learning the thought of the poet (530b10–c1), and this is picked out as especially enviable. Again, I propose that we see this instance of ironic praise as subordinate to the praise for his spending time with the poets. If this is right, the praise of Ion is the primary instance of irony, setting up the relation between Socrates and Ion qua imposter, while the further claims are ironic insofar as they support and clarify the original praise of Ion.[92] Socrates' purported envy is, in short, feigned; it is aimed at eliciting boastful claims from Ion the imposter; and it works immediately (530c7–d3, d6–8).

These boastful claims are then refuted and Ion is shown not to have a form of expertise, but Socrates continues to pretend to assume that praise is justified. The inspiration model abandons the initial claim about expertise, replacing it with a claim about inspiration, but continues to assume that Ion and rhapsodes are praiseworthy for (1) appearing beautiful and (2) spending time with poets.

---

[91] Wolfsdorf (2007) by contrast thinks that Socrates is incredibly naïve, actually believing his praise when he articulates it.

[92] The relevant praise claims are not necessarily false. The grounds for praise can be mistaken either because the praise is misapplied, in which case the thing one is praised for might really be good, or because the praise is misplaced, in which case no one ought to be praised for it.

Socrates refocuses the discussion on the poets, praising them directly. They are repeatedly praised both for being divinely inspired and for producing beautiful poetry. As I argue in Section 4, Socrates parodies the poets' self-understanding making them seem insane; if this is right, then Socrates' praise cannot be sincere and must be understood as ironic. Ion himself is not praised directly here, but this praise of the poets can be understood as an alternative specification of (1) and (2), that is, it provides another route whereby Socrates might envy Ion and the rhapsodes. For it turns out now that what is enviable about Ion is that he is possessed by a poet, Homer, who is himself possessed by the Muse, and this divine possession is what enables his beautiful appearance. In short, it is his proximity to the divine Homer that is the grounds for praising Ion. Ion himself enthusiastically endorses the praise of the poets because he takes himself to be praised by it as well. When Socrates does praise Ion directly because of the "divine gift" that makes him a "clever singer of Homer's praises" (536d3), Ion rejects it because he finally sees that the praise makes him out to be a kind of lunatic (d4–7).

When they return to the expertise model, they return to the original grounds for praise, namely expertise, and (1) appearing beautiful and (2a) understanding the poet's thought. Socrates' irony arguably takes on a more openly mocking character. He praises Ion's capacity for memorizing Homer, and then immediately wonders if he is forgetful, since Ion contradicts what he has just said (539e7–9).[93] There is also some bite in Socrates' praise of Ion's knowledge of generalship (540d–541e). Socrates primes Ion to leap at generalship, a noble and highly regarded ethical sort of expertise involving the management of people. Ion claims to have acquired this knowledge from Homer. He is praised here for a specification of (2a), but this can also be seen as an alternative specification of (1), as the rhapsode now appears in the 'beautiful,' in the sense of *noble*, guise of a general.[94] Socrates gets Ion to contradict himself almost instantly, but Ion does not see that he has been refuted. Rather, he simply accepts Ion's claim to be a general and praises Ion for being the best general in all of Greece:

SOCRATES:	And aren't you the best (*aristos*) rhapsode in Greece?
ION:	By far, Socrates.
SOCRATES:	Are you also a general, Ion? Are you the best (*aristos*) in Greece?

---

[93] Cp. *Hip. Min.* 368d–369a.
[94] In the *Republic*, generalship is described as "one of the most important and beautiful (*kallistōn*) things" that Homer speaks about (599c6–8).

ION: Certainly, Socrates. That, too, I learned from
                  Homer's poetry.

                                                    (541b2–5)

This is mockingly ironic praise, and it should be obvious to any reader of the
dialogue, even though it is not obvious to Ion. To call Ion the best (*aristos*) in
the noble (*kalos*) expertise of generalship is tantamount to saying that he
possesses virtue (*aretê*) as a human being. By assenting to this claim and
accepting the praise, Ion appears extremely foolish. After many attempts, Ion
finally gives a concrete answer to what his knowledge of Homer amounts to –
generalship – but it is a transparently ludicrous one and he is praised for it
nevertheless.

   I want to consider one final passage, in which Socrates reflects on his own
epistemic state, not merely qua ironist in relation to Ion. Socrates asks Ion if he
needs help in understanding Socrates' question, and the following exchange
ensues:

ION: Lord, yes, I do, Socrates. I love to hear you wise
                  men (*tōn sophōn*) talk.
SOCRATES: I wish what you say were true (*alēthē legein*),
                  Ion. But wise? Surely you are the wise men, you
                  rhapsodes and actors, you and the poets whose
                  works you sing. As for me, I say nothing but the
                  truth (*ouden allo ē t'alēthē*), as you'd expect it
                  from an ordinary man (*idiōtēn anthrōpon*).
                  I mean, even this question I asked you – look
                  how commonplace and ordinary (*phaulon kai
                  idiōtikon*) a matter it is. Anybody could under-
                  stand what I meant: don't you use the same
                  methodology whenever you master the whole
                  of a subject? Take this for discussion – painting
                  is a subject to be mastered as a whole, isn't it?

                                                    (532d4–e5)

There are several things to notice here: First, when Socrates departs from ironic
praise and moves on to refutation, he leads the discussion and becomes, or
reveals himself as, epistemically superior. This superiority can easily seem like
wisdom to those refuted. Second, Socrates responds to the attribution of wisdom
by immediately disavowing, as opposed to embracing, the praise. Third, he does
so at the same time as he simultaneously expresses the desire to be wise. Here
we see the philosophical side of Socratic irony, because we see at this moment
the deep and abiding contrast between the self-ignorance of Ion, which closes
off the pursuit of wisdom, and the self-knowledge of Socrates, which makes it
urgent.

Finally, Socrates ironically turns the ascription of wisdom back onto Ion, the rhapsodes, and poets and contrasts their brand of wisdom with Socrates' ordinary truth-telling. This contrast is interesting for several reasons. The contrast is between high, fancy, pleasing, dressed-up 'high' wisdom and low, ordinary, run-of-the-mill, 'low' truth.[95] One kind of knowledge redounds to the credit, esteem, and uniqueness of the purveyor, while the other is available to anyone on the street. This is an important point, since it suggests that achieving self-knowledge is possible for those who are willing to engage in philosophical conversation. Notice that Socrates does not claim here not to know anything at all, just not to possess wisdom; indeed, his claims to speak the truth seem to rely on his knowing *something*. Further, Socrates claims to speak *only* the ordinary truth in the very next sentence after ironically praising Ion, the rhapsodes, and poets as wise. This is surely irony of the dissembling sort, but it does carry with it an important moral and epistemic lesson about self-ignorance, wisdom, and philosophy: Having a self-critical attitude is the most praiseworthy way of being and the only reliable route to wisdom. Knowing one's own ignorance turns out to be a central philosophical insight that is decisive for whether one lives a good life.

6.3 Foolishness and Self-Ignorance

The philosophical purpose of the portrayal of Ion concerns diagnosing the philosophical source of his self-ignorance. Being laughable is connected to having certain commitments, and Plato thus connects his literary character to a concern with moral character. It is important to distinguish between the moral lesson for Plato's readers and the lesson that, internal to the dialogue, Socrates makes available to Ion.[96]

I begin with the moral lesson for the reader. In the middle of the dialogue, Ion emphatically claims self-knowledge (533c), that is, a stable sense of who he is and what he knows, but in the final scene Socrates compares him to Proteus, the notorious shape-shifter who avoided answering questions:[97]

> Really, you're simply just like Proteus, you twist up and down and take many different shapes, till finally you've escaped me altogether by revealing yourself as a general, so as to avoid displaying how clever (*deinos*) you are when it comes to wisdom about Homer (*tēn peri Homēron sophian*). (541e6–542a1)

---

[95] Cp. *Symp.* 221e.

[96] Often there is also an internal audience, and Socrates may have the aim of warning them about the dangers of taking his interlocutor as a teacher: see, e.g., *Rep.* and *Prot.*

[97] See, e.g., Homer, *Od.* 4.385ff.

Ion has happily accepted being an expert, being a divinely inspired interpreter, and finally being a general, so long as he gets to hold on to his central claim to be an authority on Homer. What he has not been able to do is consistently explain what exactly it is he knows about Homer. Unlike Proteus, Ion is not changing identities because he is trying to hide what he really knows or who he really is but because he does not know what he really knows and who he really is. He is thus genuinely laughable because of a particular vice, self-ignorance. Yet Ion is not merely self-ignorant – he has a shifting and unstable self-conception. It is important then to see how this particular form of self-ignorance is connected to Ion's central commitment to knowledge of Homer. Indeed, the very basis for his claim about self-knowledge turns out to be the main source of his self-ignorance.

Ion's core mistake is to treat Homer as a source of wisdom and to think of himself as possessing wisdom on the basis of Homer. The clearest piece of evidence for this is Ion's emphatic claim to have generalship from Homer: "That too, I learned from Homer!" (541b4–5). Note that Ion's formulation strongly suggests here that there are many other things he has learned from Homer. He puts himself in a passive epistemic relation to Homer, and this passivity involves or entails other, more general epistemological commitments. We see these commitments, and thus the forms of Ion's self-ignorance, played out differently in the rhapsode's roles as performer and interpreter.

As interpreter, Ion is committed to the claim that knowledge can be acquired through acquaintance with poetry. Ion "spends time with" Homer in the manner of a pupil listening to lectures. In short, it is the move from knowing about Homer to knowing what Homer knows that grounds Ion's claim to expertise. However, Socrates exposes the gap between these two in the dialogue. By comparing Ion's alleged Homer-based expertise unfavorably to the expertise of those who actually learned their craft, Ion is repeatedly shown, or forced to admit, that he doesn't really know what the experts know. This, however, does not yet capture the extent of Ion's epistemic error, for he also seems to think that having acquired expertise through Homer puts him in a position to *evaluate* Homer's knowledge as superior and thus to praise it. This evaluation of Homer as superior is completely unfounded. It relies either on a prior assumption about Homer's superiority or on the fact that Ion experiences Homer's poetry as more engaging. Yet one deceives oneself in thinking that one can gain knowledge by learning the lines of Homer, and one ends up looking like a fool. This is not a lesson restricted to Ion or to rhapsodes but one with general significance for Plato's readership.

As performer, Ion thinks that knowledge can be acquired passively by compellingly performing the actions of experts, that is, by imitating them and thus appearing to be noble or fine. He thus mistakes himself for the characters he plays.[98] Ion's shape-shifting is not merely a function of his lack of skill in rational argumentation; it is rather an ability that is enabled by his performances. When Ion reveals himself as the best general in all of Greece, he is committed to an arguably deeper mistake about the relation between knowledge and appearance. Just as he thinks that he speaks well about Homer on the basis of appearing to his audience to speak well, so too he thinks that he can do the job of a general well on the basis of compellingly appearing to be a great general in his performances. The claim seems to be that the ability to imitate persuasively requires knowledge; a corollary of this is that general audiences, that is, non-experts, can correctly identify expertise from its appearance. Ion can thus mistake himself for all of the different roles that he inhabits in the Homeric universe. This is connected to a broader claim about beauty and nobility, that is, what is *kalos*, since Ion seems to think that there is nothing more to being *kalos* than seeming *kalos*.[99] If that is right, then the best general will be the one who seems best to some audience. The lesson for readers is not just, more narrowly, that rhapsodes and actors are not wise but that the compelling appearance of wisdom is not sufficient for the possession of wisdom and the compelling appearance of nobility is not sufficient for genuine nobility. There is a further lesson here, however, since we still have not addressed the more basic question of why Ion thinks that Homer is a source of wisdom to begin with. I submit that this is simply an extension of the same epistemic mistake, thinking that Homer's ability to produce poetry that compellingly reproduces the activities of carpenters, generals, and statesmen requires that he himself possess knowledge of such matters.[100] This lesson is of utmost concern for a culture that assumes that Homer is a source of knowledge.

In sum, Ion's identity crisis – his self-ignorance and lack of stable self-conception – is connected to particular epistemic mistakes he makes in relation to Homer. He does know at least one thing though. He has memorized and can recite the poetry of Homer. Yet this is not, in itself, a form of expertise, and Ion, like the craftsman described in the *Apology*, mistakenly infers, on the basis of what he does know, that he knows a bunch of other matters of ethical and political import. Ion thinks himself to "be most wise in other respects" (22c5–6; cp. 22d) on the basis of his cleverness about Homer. Readers should not make the same foolish mistake.

Turning to the internal educational dynamics of the dialogue, I want to argue briefly that Socrates attempts to improve Ion morally and that his failure to

---

[98] Cp. Ar. *Ach.* 410–415; *Th.* 149–150.

[99] On Hippias' similar mistake in *Hip. Ma.*, see Trivigno (2016).   [100] Cp. *Rep.* 598e.

improve him is not for lack of effort. One might worry that, according to my reading, Socrates simply tricks Ion into making outrageous claims and then just hangs him out to dry. To formulate this worry more sharply, Socrates deceives Ion into thinking that Socrates admires him; he does so in order to elicit extravagant claims to knowledge; he elicits these claims in order to make Ion seem ridiculous; and, at the end of the dialogue, Ion seems hardly to have understood anything and goes away from the conversation thinking of himself as blessed by the gods. Since there is no audience of onlookers who might have been benefited by seeing Ion treated this way, we seem to be left with the unpleasant conclusion that Socrates deceives and harms Ion just for fun.

On my reading, Ion misses Socrates' irony because he *already* thinks highly of himself, is eager to be praised, and is thus primed to accept praise. Socrates thus does deceive Ion, praising Ion to draw out knowledge-claims, but these claims are ones that Ion already *implicitly* believes. Socrates elicits their explicit formulation in order to put them to the test. It is this testing of knowledge-claims that holds the potential for Ion's moral improvement. For, by being refuted, that is, being shown that he lacks the knowledge that he claims to have, Ion may be led from having self-ignorance, not knowing what he knows and does not know, to having self-knowledge and thus seeing the deep need for philosophical investigation.[101] Socrates certainly tries to get Ion to see, and thus reveal, himself repeatedly in the dialogue. Consider the passage in which Socrates imagines that it is Ion asking Socrates about which passages belong to the diviner (538d7). Socrates is both attributing to Ion a question on the basis of his previous answers to Socrates' questions and nevertheless making Ion imagine asking a question that he would never actually ask, since it involves conceding that he is not the expert on Homer that he makes himself out to be. Or consider the passage where Socrates denies that Ion's answer really is *his* answer: "You, Ion, do not say 'all of them'" (539e7). Thus, Socrates attempts to put Ion before himself for examination. Though Ion does not benefit directly from the irony and deception, he benefits from the refutation that reveals that his self-ignorance, shows him who he really is, and points the way for how he might become better. Thus, the deception of Socratic irony is instrumental to truth and ethical benefit.

This strategic use of deception is paternalistic, but, given Plato's defense of noble lies elsewhere,[102] it would be hard to argue that he would find such improvement strategies ethically repugnant. Ion really is laughable, and he

---

[101] Cp. Socrates' conversations in the *Meno*, *Charmides*, and *Alcibiades I*.

[102] Cp. *Rep.* 389b7–9 on the appropriate poetic tales: "Then if it is appropriate for anyone to use falsehoods for the good of the city, because of the actions of either enemies or citizens, it is the rulers."

cannot escape this condition if he is blissfully unaware of it. Of course, this makes the question of what, if anything, Ion has learned from the discussion even more pressing. Ion leaves the discussion thinking that its upshot is that he is 'divine,' suggesting that he has learned nothing. Yet Ion has at least learned that his abilities with respect to Homer are not a function of expertise but of divine dispensation – which he should count himself lucky to receive. This may not be true in the sense that is articulated in the inspiration model, but it is still a lot closer to the truth than the claim that he has expertise. Even if Ion has learned nothing further, Socrates' refutation of him at least makes it *possible* for Ion to see his own situation more clearly. The fact that Ion refuses to do so is hardly Socrates' fault.

7 The Critical Engagement Model

One might think that the foregoing analysis of the dialogue is really all that needs to be said about the *Ion*. Neither rhapsodes nor poets have any knowledge, and any true claims that make their way into poetry are the result of luck. We should be careful to avoid making Ion-like mistakes that will turn us into self-ignorant fools. In the end, we should just ignore poetry. This would perhaps be the safest position to take. However, I think that there are at least two good reasons to think that there is more to be said. First, Plato doesn't ignore poetry. He quotes, references, and engages with poetry extensively in his dialogues. As Halliwell nicely puts it, Plato's "engagement with the culturally powerful texts and voices of poetry is so evident, so persistent, and so intense as to constitute a major thread running through the entire fabric of his writing and thinking" (2000, 94).[103] So Plato does not himself simply ignore poetry, and this demands explanation. Second, during the course of the *Ion*, Socrates seems to endorse both the expertise model at 532d8, when he says "I speak nothing but the truth," and the inspiration model at 534b3, when he says, of the poet's descriptions of inspiration, "what they say is true."[104] These emphatic assertions of truth suggest that there may be something salvageable from each account. My guiding questions are the following: Can poetry contain true content, and under what conditions might it do so? Is there a way to gain any epistemic benefit from poetry, and under what conditions might this be possible?

Looking for a positive view on these matters again requires us to think beyond what is offered explicitly in the text. One way to start to think about what aspects of each account are salvageable is to try to identify mistakes

---

[103] Cp. Tarrant (1951).

[104] These truth-assertions might be explained away, but I think that explaining away emphatic assertions of truth should be an interpretive move of last resort, so I will attempt to make sense of them.

common to both accounts, so that these can be ruled out. It seems clear that both accounts assume a privileged role for the poet. Both accounts assume that the rhapsode is the vehicle by which audiences can gain access to the poet's privileged position. Both thus offer systematic attempts to describe why poets are appropriately revered and why rhapsodes are extremely useful. I think it is safe to set these claims aside as unpromising starting points. I will argue instead that the dialogue is consistent with a version of the inspiration model for non-knowledge-based poetry and a version of the expertise model as an *ideal* for poetry that is based on expertise. In both cases, what is necessary is the audience's critical engagement.

7.1 Poetry As Potentially Inspired

The analogy between divination and poetry is very prominent in Socrates' articulation of the inspiration model. However, in that model, it makes poets implausibly mindless vehicles of a kind of beauty that causes audience decep-tion. Thus, it seems to fail both as an explanation of poetic success and as an account of how one ought to relate to poetry, and it seems to leave content almost entirely out of the picture. One motivation for trying to revive a version of the inspiration account is because we find versions of it prominently asserted in a number of other dialogues. This does not entail that we must simply accept the inspiration model, as articulated, but it does give us grounds for seeing whether a modified version of it might be defensible. In this section, I show how Plato uses divine inspiration as an explanation of non-knowledge-based suc-cess, and I use this paradigm to show how poetry might be understood as inspired insofar as it contains true content and can benefit the audience. In this way, poetry can be seen as comparable to an oracle. Following Socrates' example, we ought to test and examine, rather than passively accept, the oracle's message, that is, subject it to philosophical scrutiny.

Plato connects poets to divine inspiration in several places in his corpus.[105] In the *Apology*, Socrates says that the poets "say many fine things (*polla kai kala*) without any understanding of what they say" (22c2–3). Plato also attributes divine inspiration to prophets and, in general, to agents who have epistemic success without knowledge. The *Meno* is most helpful for elucidating this point: Socrates is trying to explain how it could be the case that good and successful politicians were not able to teach their own sons to be good and successful. The explanation is that they did not have wisdom or knowledge but "right opinion" (99b11). Like soothsayers, prophets, and poets, such politicians "say many true things (*alēthē kai polla*) when inspired, but they have no knowledge of what they are saying" (99c3–5). We "call these men divine" because they "are right (*katorthousin*) in much that is of importance in what they say and do" and "their speeches lead to success in many important matters, though they have no knowledge of what they are saying," and the explanation of this is that they are inspired by the gods (99c7–d5). What I find illuminating and helpful in this passage is the guidance it provides in figuring out what kind of success divine inspiration might be used to explain. In the *Meno* passage, the gods are credited for the true claims that are made and the successful outcomes that result from the statesman's speeches. In short, divine inspiration can explain real success, not just success within a restricted domain given certain egoistic goals.

Turning to the case of poetry, I think this paradigm tells against thinking of divine inspiration as what explains the poet's ability to achieve merely superficial beauty, captivate audiences, and win contests. As I analyze it in Section 5.2, superficial beauty is characterized by deceptiveness, and this usually redounds to the economic benefit of the performer and plausibly harms the audience. I find it very difficult to believe that Plato could seriously make the gods the causal agent of harmful deceptiveness. An axiom of Platonic theology, if one can talk in these terms, is that the gods are good and the cause of only good.[106] It seems more reasonable to think that divine inspiration explains the presence of true beauty in poetry, for example true content about virtue and goodness, or, as in the case of politicians, the achievement of ethical benefit to audiences. This suggests understanding the 'many beautiful things' of the *Apology* as equivalent to the 'many true things' of the *Meno*. Poetry, then, can contain true claims that are not defended or argued for in the text, and the god is responsible for the presence of these claims. Like the *Meno*'s politicians, who cannot teach their own sons to be good, the poets cannot be teachers, even when their poetry contains true claims about important matters (cp. *Ap.* 22b–c). Nor indeed can rhapsodes, even when they happen to perform poetry that has divinely inspired content.[107] In the cases where the beauty is partly constitutive of the content, the gods may be responsible for this aspect of its beauty as well. The poets need not be *entirely* passive, as in the inspiration model, but passive with respect to the content of the poetry. They will be in no position to distinguish between true and false content and never know about themselves whether they are composing verses that are inspired or not. This might indicate a division of labor between poet and gods, such that the former is responsible for the form, whereas the

---

[106] See esp. *Rep.* 379a–c; *Laws* 901d–e, 906b.

[107] Cp. Xen. *Symp.* 4.6, where Niceratus claims to be able to improve others on the basis of knowledge gained from Homer.

latter are responsible for the content, of divinely inspired poetry.[108] In the case
of a superficially beautiful and gripping presentation of false content, the god is
not involved. One upshot of this reading is that it makes very good sense of
Plato's robust engagement with poetry. Sometimes poetry gets some important
truths right, and this explains why Plato seems to take some *poetry* seriously.
However, since the source of the truth is the gods, he need not therefore take
poets seriously.

Poems, then, can contain true and beautiful claims, and we have an explanation for how this is possible that does not impart wisdom to the poets. Yet not
all poetic utterances can be inspired, since the poets say contradictory things.[109]
Indeed, according to the inspiration model, only some poets are inspired and
only some of the time. This suggests that the gods selectively inspire the poets,
and poetry will never by itself be a reliable guide to truth. Yet if poetry is an
unreliable guide to truth, how could we know which poems are inspired and
which not? Failing some way of finding out, is it not safer that we just ignore it?
Building on the analogy with divination and Socrates' own way of responding
to the oracle at Delphi (*Ap*. 21a–23b), I claim that rational, critical engagement
is the proper way both to find out whether some poetic utterance was inspired
and to understand its general significance. Consider the following description of
divination in the *Timaeus*:

> While he is in his right mind (*ennous*), no one engages in divination,
> however divinely inspired and true it may be, but only when his power
> of understanding is bound in sleep or by sickness, or when some sort of
> possession works a change in him. On the other hand, it takes a man who
> has his wits about him (*emphronos*) to recall and comprehend (*sunnoēsai*)
> the pronouncements produced by this state of divination or possession,
> whether in sleep or while awake. It takes such a man to rationally analyze
> (*logismōi dielesthai*) any and all visions to determine how and for whom
> they signify some future, past or present good or evil. But as long as the fit
> remains on him, the man is incompetent to render judgment on his own
> visions and voices. As the ancient proverb well puts it, "Only a man of
> sound mind (*sōphroni*) may know himself and conduct his own affairs."
> This is the reason why it is customary practice to appoint prophets to render
> judgment on an inspired divination. (71e3–72b1)

---

[108] *Pace* Woodruff (1982, 145), I do not find the idea impossible, though I do see that it is
problematic.

[109] Indeed, one might object that *Laws* 719c–d seems to tell against my suggestion, since it
describes the same poet as "often obliged to contradict himself" (719c7). However, what
explains the self-contradiction is the poet's need to imitate contrary characters. Divine inspiration might still explain the true claims that are made, even though the poet will not know which
one that is.

In the context of the passage, a distinction between a seer and a prophet is being articulated, making the process of divination require both inspired vision and rational analysis and interpretation. This passage is highly reminiscent of, and relevant for, the *Ion* in at least three ways: its contrast between being inspired and thus out of one's mind and being in one's right mind and capable of rational thought; its combination of divine inspiration and rational interpretation; and its understanding of the passivity of the seer as a kind of self-ignorance. For my purposes, what is most revealing is the idea that the message of the god is inaccessible – it cannot be comprehended – unless it is subject to rational analysis. Without that, the divine message cannot give us any guidance on how to live and what to do.

The *Timaeus* passage fits rather well Socrates' own description of how he handled the Oracle at Delphi's proclamation that no one is wiser than he is (*Ap.* 21a). Socrates, well aware that he knows nothing important and is thus not wise, treats the god's message as a "riddle" (21b4) and engages in an "investigation" aimed at finding a counterexample, that is, a person wiser then himself, so that he could "refute the oracle" (21b8–c1). This investigation revealed that, as a matter of fact, Socrates was wiser than everyone else not because he possessed divine wisdom, or wisdom about goodness and virtue, but because all of the others were self-ignorant, thinking wrongly that they were wise, while he had self-knowledge, understanding that he himself did not possess wisdom (20d–e, 23a–a). In short, he subjects the divine proclamation to rational scrutiny, and the oracle's deeper significance only emerges after much intellectual toil. The *source* or genesis of the oracle's truth is in the god, who "does not lie" (21b6), but the *justification* for the oracle's truth is the argument and rational analysis provided by Socrates.[110]

How might this apply to the interpretation of poetry? One can treat poetic utterances as riddles that need to be investigated rationally. Such rational testing will involve the attempt to refute, or disprove, the content of the poem. As in the case of Socrates' conversations with his interlocutors, this rational process might require some initial clarifying in order to make the utterance an appropriate object for rational analysis. Further, as in the case of the understanding of the oracle, one might end up with an interpretation that distinguishes between a surface meaning, available at the beginning of the process, and a deeper meaning, available only at the end.[111] We can never know, in advance, which poetic utterances are divinely inspired, so the conclusion that a particular poetic

---

[110] The gods would presumably know the justification, but divine messages do not, all by themselves, provide it.

[111] Might all poetic utterances be made to say something true? This seems to me to be clearly ruled out by the fact that the poets contradict each other and themselves (*Laws* 719c–d), and it fits

utterance does contain truth provides the only kind of evidence that we can hope for. This uncertainty means that the interpretation and analysis of poetry can never be a primary mode of philosophical inquiry.[112] It can never replace, or compete with, dialectical conversation aimed at truth. However, since one knows that some poetry contains divinely inspired truth, one can use poetry as a kind of proxy dialogue partner. If a verse of poetry is found by this rational method to be inspired, then one may also justifiably appeal to it in a conversation with others as inspired by the gods, since that turns out to be the only viable explanation for how true content got there to begin with. If it turns out that the poem was not inspired, since it contains a false view to be rejected, this is by no means problematic. Indeed, the testing and refutation of false claims can hardly be said to harm Socrates, who quite plausibly benefits from it. Thus, critical engagement is the only way that spending time with the poets may be valuable, and so the interpretation of poetry requires not a rhapsode but a philosopher.

7.2 The Possibility of Knowledge-Based Poetry

I now turn to the possibility of knowledge-based poetry, that is, poetry that has been informed by knowledge. Nothing I have said so far rules out this possibility. What is ruled out is the idea that the poet possesses technical knowledge and ethical wisdom in virtue of being a poet. I consider two versions of the possibility of knowledge-based poetry: The first considers the possibility that a poet possesses some specific expertise and writes poetry that contains true opinions regarding that form of expertise; whereas the second, more like inspired poetry, considers the possibility that some other expert provides the poet with true opinions. In both cases, some epistemic agent's knowledge is what explains the presence of true content in the poem.

I take the first kind of case to be allowed implicitly by the argument towards the end of the dialogue in which Socrates asks Ion in virtue of what it is that he would know what a general should say. Socrates considers the possibility that Ion is both a rhapsode and a general and that the latter explains how he knows the "business of a general" (540e7):

> SOCRATES: I mean, if you were somehow both a horseman
>   and a cithara-player at the same time, you would
>   know good riders from bad. But suppose I asked

---

poorly with the picture of inspiration in the *Ion* as selective rather than ubiquitous. See my discussion of this issue in Trivigno (2013, 526).

[112] See Trivigno (2013, 539–541).

you: "Which profession teaches you good horsemanship – the one that makes you a horseman, or
the one that makes you a cithara-player?"
ION: The horseman, I'd say.

(540d6–e4)

There is no reason to deny, and every reason to affirm, the possibility that
one might have some other expertise in addition to being a poet. Plato would
have had the very prominent example of Solon, who was both a legislator
and a poet. For the example to work, one would need to be able to write
poetry that somehow contained the content from another discipline. Since
poetry is repeatedly treated as a form of speaking with epistemic content,
I see no obstacle in principle to a single individual setting the content of
some discipline into verse form. As in the case of inspired poetry, what is
gained from the poem is still not knowledge but true opinion. Even if the
poet somehow builds the structure of justification into the poem, one could
not passively accept and receive knowledge from the poem just by memorizing it. Thus, knowledge would still be accessible only through a process of
rational testing. Since nonexperts would not be able to judge whether the
poet who claimed to be a general really possessed generalship, one would
need to test the claim in order to find out whether it was informed by
knowledge to begin with.

The other possibility for knowledge-based poetry would involve cooperation
between the poet and someone else who had the relevant knowledge. Socrates
does not directly countenance this possibility, but I see no reason to think that
such a division of labor is ruled out by anything Socrates does say. On this
picture, the relevant expert could provide the poet with the appropriate right
opinions that the latter might include and/or endorse in the poem. Alternatively,
the expert could correct or edit the poem's content for accuracy and correctness.
In neither case does the expert need to teach the poet the relevant expertise, in
the sense of explaining to the poet *why* the opinions are justified and how they fit
together to comprise the discipline. As in the above example, we would have
a knowledge-based explanation for how true opinions are present in poetry; and,
as above, it is true opinion, not knowledge, that the audience gets from the
poetry, and one cannot become knowledgeable simply by becoming acquainted
with even this knowledge-based poetry. The claims still need to be tested and
examined in order to attain actual knowledge. The proposal of the *Republic* that
the philosophers supervise the poets when it comes to the ethical or moral
content of poetry is a good example of cooperation between a poet and one with
expertise (377b–c). Even when nonexpert citizens can basically be certain that
the content will be true, one still only acquires true opinions and not knowledge,

because one does not yet understand the reason why the opinions are true.[113]
Since the process of achieving genuine understanding necessarily involves the
articulation and rebuttal of possible objections, critical engagement will still be
necessary.

One might object at this point that I have been implicitly treating poetry here
as itself a form of expertise. Is this justified and what exactly would such an
expertise have as its proper content? The answer, I am afraid, is unclear, and my
formulations in this section have been intentionally noncommittal. As I argue in
this Element, the whole thrust of the dialogue tells against the idea that poetry is,
as a matter of fact, a form of expertise practiced by actual poets; however, this
does not necessarily rule out the possibility that poetry might be a form of
expertise that some ideal poets might practice. Socrates at one point affirms that
"there is an art of poetry (*poiētikē*) as a whole (*to holon*)" (532c8–9), and one
might understand this as descriptively false, since there actually is no such craft,
but ideally true, since there could be. One candidate for poetic expertise, namely
versification, can be ruled out fairly safely.[114] The reason is twofold: First, while
Plato speaks often about poetry, its goals, epistemic status, and effects, he never
countenances the possibility that the setting of content into verse is itself a form
of expertise. Further, there is good reason to think that Plato would positively
reject the proposal. In the *Phaedrus*, Socrates argues that the techniques of
rhetoric, just like the techniques of tragedy and medicine, are the "preliminary"
(269a) aspects of these crafts but not the crafts themselves (268c–269a). In
short, by a parity of argument, Plato would have considered versification to be
a necessary condition of poetry but not what poetry itself consists in. In the
Apology at least, the possibility is raised that one might simply have a natural or
inborn talent for poetry (22b–c).

Two more promising candidates for what the alleged craft of poetry might
consist in are the production of images, as analogous to painting, and the
making of claims, as analogous to rhetoric. This does not solve our issue
because, in both the case of painting and rhetoric, it is unclear whether Plato
thinks that these are, or could be, crafts. In the *Phaedrus* and *Statesman*, for
example, rhetoric is granted the status of a craft, whereas the *Gorgias* seems
only to allow that rhetoric might eventually become a craft, arguing that it is, as
practiced, merely a knack. Another way to think about the question is to ask
what the *ergon*, or function, of the alleged poetic expertise might be, or what its
telos or end is. Here, Plato is consistent in attributing to poetry two competing
ends with respect to the audience: either the goal of poetry is to cause the

---

[113] In both *Republic* and the *Laws*, an ideal city is described in which poetry, whose content is
strictly supervised by the state, is made essential to the education of the citizens.

[114] *Pace* Janaway (1995); Trivigno (2012a).

audience to feel pleasurable emotions or the goal of poetry to is educate the audience. Plato is at least consistent in denying that causing the audience pleasure could qualify as an expertise. He rather classifies such activities as knacks, that is, as the unscientific repetition of previous successful strategies that lacks an understanding of the nature of its subject matter (*Grg.* 465a). Educating the audience could be done scientifically, but that would require an understanding of the nature of the soul (*Phdr.* 271a–b).

8 Conclusion

In this Element, I have argued that Plato's *Ion* is primarily concerned with audience reception of poetry. On my reading, the dialogue countenances and rejects two models of poetic reception, the expertise model and the inspiration model, and it presents the character of Ion as a comedic figure, an imposter, whose foolishness is a function of his passive relation to Homer and his poetry. In the end, I suggested that critical engagement is the proper way for audiences to treat poetry. This view holds open the possibility that poetry may express some truths without thereby endorsing the idea that poets are experts who have authoritative knowledge. I hope that philosophical interest of my final speculative remarks has provided some indirect support for my hermeneutical approach. If I were to assume that one must stick to the letter of the dialogue and claims found therein, then I would not be able to argue for anything beyond a negative conclusion about the rhapsodic *technē*. One would thus miss out on the philosophical richness of the dialogue. Further, I take it that my own interpretation is in the spirit of the model it seeks to defend. In short, I have applied the critical engagement model to the interpretation of Plato, for there is no reason to think that his works would be able to transmit knowledge to a passive audience. If there is knowledge to be had, we have to go after it ourselves.[115]

---

[115] I would like to thank Ingvild Torsen, Reidar Maliks, David Ebrey, James Warren and an anonymous reviewer for their helpful criticisms and feedback.

References

Brickhouse, Thomas and Nicholas Smith (1994). *Plato's Socrates*. Oxford: Oxford University Press.

Cooper, John M., ed. (1997). *Plato: Complete Works*. Indianapolis: Hackett.

Cornford, Francis (1961). *The Origin of Attic Comedy*. Garden City, NY: Anchor.

Diggle, James (2004). *Theophrastus: Characters*. Cambridge: Cambridge University Press.

Dorter, Kenneth (1973). "The Ion: Plato's Characterization of Art," *The Journal of Aesthetics and Art Criticism* 32, 65–78.

Ferrari, Giovanni R. F. (2008). "Socratic Irony as Pretence." *Oxford Studies in Ancient Philosophy* 34, 1–33.

Flashar, Helmus (1958). *Der Dialog Ion als Zeugnis platonischer Philosophie*. Berlin: Akademie-Verlag.

Greene, William (1918). "Plato's View of Poetry." *Harvard Studies in Classical Philology* 19, 1–75.

Grene, David and Richard Lattimore (1959). *Euripides V: Electra; The Phoenician Women; The Bacchae*. Chicago: University of Chicago Press.

Halliwell, Stephen (2000). "The Subjection of *Muthos* to *Logos*: Plato's Citations of the Poets," *Classical Quarterly* 50, 94–112.

Havelock, Eric A. (1963). *Preface to Plato*. Cambridge, MA: Harvard University Press.

Janaway, Christopher (1995). *Images of Excellence: Plato's Critique of the Arts*. Oxford: Clarendon Press.

LaDrière, Craig (1951). "The Problem of Plato's *Ion*," *Journal of Aesthetics and Art Criticism* 10, 26–34.

Lane, Melissa (2006). "The Evolution of *Eironeia* in Classical Greek Texts: Why Socratic *Eironeia* is Not Irony." *Oxford Studies in Ancient Philosophy* 31, 49–83.

Lear, Gabriel Richardson (2006). "Plato on Learning to Love Beauty," in Gerasimos Santas (ed.), *The Blackwell Guide to Plato's Republic*. Oxford: Blackwell 104–24.

MacDowell, Douglas (1990). "The Meaning of *Alazon*," in E. M. Craik (ed.), *Owls to Athens*. Oxford, Oxford University Press, 287–292.

Moore, John (1974). "The Dating of Plato's *Ion*," *Greek, Roman and Byzantine Studies* 15, 421–440.

Moss, Jessica (2012). "Art and Ethical Perspective: Notes on the *Kalon* in Plato's *Laws*," in Alison Denham (ed.), *Plato on Art and Beauty*. London: Palgrave Macmillan, 205–220.

Murray, Penelope (1992). "Inspiration and Mimesis in Plato," in Andrew Barker and Martin Warner (eds.), *The Language of the Cave*. Edmonton: Academic Printing & Publishing, 27–46.

Murray Penelope, ed. (1996). *Plato on Poetry*. Cambridge: Cambridge University Press.

Nightingale, Andrea (1995). *Genres in Dialogue*. Cambridge: Cambridge University Press.

Pappas, Nicholas (1989). "Plato's 'Ion': The Problem of the Author," *Philosophy* 64, 381–389.

Radford, Colin (1975). "How Can We Be Moved by the Fate of Anna Karenina?" *Proceedings of the Aristotelian Society* 49, 67–80.

Ranta, Jerrald (1967). "The Drama of Plato's 'Ion,'" *Journal of Aesthetics and Art Criticism* 26, 219–229.

Richardson, Nicholas J. (2006). "Homeric Professors in the Age of the Sophists," in Andrew Laird (ed.), *Oxford Readings in Classical Studies: Ancient Literary Criticism*. Oxford: Oxford University Press, 62–86.

Rijksbaron, Albert (2007). *Plato: Ion or On the Iliad*. Leiden: Brill.

Stern-Gillet, Suzanne (2004). "On (mis)interpreting Plato's *Ion*." *Phronesis* 49, 169–201.

Tarrant, Dorothy (1951). "Plato's Use of Quotations and Other Illustrative Material," *Classical Quarterly* 45, 59–67.

Thesleff, Holger (2009). *Platonic Patterns*. Las Vegas: Parmenides Publishing.

Tigerstedt, E. N. (1969). *Plato's Idea of Poetical Inspiration*. Helsinki: Societas Scientiarum Fennica.

Trivigno, Franco V. (2009a). "The Rhetoric of Parody in Plato's *Menexenus*," *Philosophy and Rhetoric* 42, 29–58.

Trivigno, Franco V. (2009b). "Putting Unity in Its Place: Organic Unity in Plato's *Phaedrus*," *Literature and Aesthetics* 19: 153–182.

Trivigno, Franco V. (2011a). "Philosophy and the Ordinary: On the Setting of Plato's *Lysis*," *Greek, Roman and Byzantine Studies*, 51, 61–85.

Trivigno, Franco V. (2011b). "Is Good Tragedy Possible? The Argument of *Gorgias* 502b–503b," *Oxford Studies in Ancient Philosophy* 41, 115–138.

Trivigno, Franco V. (2012a). "Technê, Inspiration and Comedy in Plato's Ion," *Apeiron* 45, 283–313.

Trivigno, Franco V. (2012b). "Etymology and the Power of Names in Plato's *Cratylus*," *Ancient Philosophy* 32, 35–75.

Trivigno, Franco V. (2013). "Childish Nonsense? The Value of Interpretation in Plato's *Protagoras*," *Journal of the History of Philosophy* 51, 509–543.

Trivigno, Franco V. (2016). "The Moral and the Literary Character of Hippias in the *Hippias Major*," *Oxford Studies in Ancient Philosophy* 50, 31–65.

Trivigno, Franco V. (2017). "A Doctor's Folly: Diagnosing the Speech of Eryximachus," in Pierre Destrée and Zina Giannopoulou (eds.), *Plato's Symposium: A Critical Guide*. Cambridge: Cambridge University Press, 48–69.

Urmson, J. O. (1982). "Plato and the Poets," in Julius Moravcsik and Philip Temko (eds.), *Plato on Beauty, Wisdom and the Arts*. Lanham, MD: Rowman and Littlefield, 125–136.

Vasiliou, Iakovos (1999). "Conditional Irony in the Socratic Dialogues," *Classical Quarterly* 49, 456–472.

Vlastos, Gregory (1991). *Socrates, Ironist and Moral Philosopher*. Ithaca, NY: Cornell University Press.

Wolfsdorf, David (2007). "The Irony of Socrates," *The Journal of Aesthetics and Art Criticism* 65, 176–187.

Woodruff, Paul (1982). "What Could Go Wrong with Inspiration? Why Plato's Poets Fail," in Julius Moravcsik and Philip Temko (eds.), *Plato on Beauty, Wisdom and the Arts*. Lanham, MD: Rowman and Littlefield, 137–150.

Woolf, Raphael. (1997). "The Self in Plato's Ion," *Apeiron* 30, 189–210.

Cambridge Elements ☰

Ancient Philosophy

James Warren
University of Cambridge

James Warren is Professor of Ancient Philosophy at the University of Cambridge. He is the author of *Epicurus and Democritean Ethics* (Cambridge, 2002), *Facing Death: Epicurus and his Critics* (2004), *Presocratics* (2007), *The Pleasures of Reason in Plato, Aristotle and the Hellenistic Hedonists* (Cambridge, 2014). He is also the editor of *The Cambridge Companion to Epicurus* (Cambridge, 2009), and joint editor of *Authors and Authorities in Ancient Philosophy* (Cambridge, 2018).

About the Series

The Elements in Ancient Philosophy series deals with a wide variety of topics and texts in ancient Greek and Roman philosophy, written by leading scholars in the field. Taking a theme, question, or type of argument, some Elements explore it across antiquity and beyond. Others look in detail at an ancient author, a specific work, or a part of a longer work, considering its structure, content, and significance, or explore more directly ancient perspectives on modern philosophical questions.

Cambridge Elements ≡

Ancient Philosophy

Elements in the Series

A full series listing is available at: www.cambridge.org/EIAP

CPSIA information can be obtained
at www.ICGtesting.com
Printed in the USA
LVHW052023071120
671044LV00008B/149